Typewriting

Pitmans College

CORONET BOOKS
Hodder Paperbacks Ltd., London

First published 1947 by
The English Universities Press Ltd.
Coronet Edition 1972

Printed in Great Britain
for Coronet Books, Hodder Paperbacks Ltd.,
St. Paul's House, Warwick Lane, London, E.C.4,
by Richard Clay (The Chaucer Press), Ltd.,
Bungay, Suffolk

ISBN 0 340 16046 2

CONTENTS

INTRODUCTION

" Teach Yourself Typewriting " has been specially prepared for those who are unable or find it inconvenient to attend recognised training centres for personal tuition in the subject.

A good knowledge of touch typewriting can be acquired within a reasonable period, but it is necessary to impress upon would-be typists that the skill is not one that can be acquired without considerable effort on their part.

The typewriting skill required by the majority of typists is efficient keyboard operation at reasonable speeds (and, incidentally, it must be emphasised that accuracy should not be sacrificed to speed); ability to decipher manuscript; the preparation of correspondence; and the capacity to set out effectively a piece of tabular or display work.

In this book these and other aspects of the subject have received careful attention. For those who wish to continue their study of typewriting from the public examination point of view or from the teaching angle, there are many standard works on those particular branches of the subject.

The instruction in keyboard mastery is based on the method of memorising or locating the keyboard row by row and subsequently as a whole—a method approved by leading authorities on typewriting and one by which excellent results have been achieved.

Many undergoing this course of instruction will not be particularly concerned with high speed in typewriting. A fair working speed for the ordinary typist is one in the neighbourhood of 50–60 words a minute. There is a section consisting of speed tests, and in it an explanation is given of what constitutes a word when an examination is being undertaken.

There is also an important section containing facsimile typewritten documents, and it is confidently believed that those carrying out the scheme of work set out in this book will have, on completion, a knowledge of typewriting that will meet the demands of most businesses and professions.

SECTION I

TOUCH TYPEWRITING

SINCE the days of the early typewriters (interesting examples of which can be seen at the Science Museum, South Kensington, London) there have been remarkable developments and improvements in the manufacture of typewriters. Many different models are now available, including portable typewriters weighing as little as 9 lb.; noiseless machines for those whose work is likely to disturb other people; and electrically operated models, which produce a particularly clear typescript. Typewriters can be obtained with different symbols for specialised work. These developments have contributed largely to the efficient conduct of administrative work connected with business enterprises and the various professions.

There has also been great progress in typewriting instruction, due in large part to the provision of better equipment, and also to the many excellent textbooks prepared specially for both students and teachers.

The "Sight" Typist

Before the teaching of typewriting received adequate attention in schools and colleges throughout the country, the majority of typists were compelled to resort to what was known as the "sight" (or visual) method, and many of them did not use all the fingers of each hand for keyboard operation. Although reasonably good work was performed by those not trained in the "touch" method, a tremendous amount of physical energy was expended by them unnecessarily in the production of their typewritten work.

The Touch Method

This method has played an important part in typewriting progress, as it is based on scientific principles. It renders unnecessary continual movement of the eyes from keyboard to copy and from copy to keyboard, as the operator finds the correct key by location and not by sight. The system relies upon the sense of location coupled with the memorising of the keyboard, and, when the typist becomes expert, keyboard work is almost a mechanical or subconscious operation. The word " touch " cannot be applied in its strictest interpretation. It is not that sense of touch by which a blind reader, for instance, identifies the raised braille characters; for each key on the typewriter keyboard " feels " the same.

Basis of Touch Typewriting

The basis of touch typewriting is that each finger operates only those keys allotted to it. Mental confusion and eyestrain are avoided, as the fingers are properly trained to respond accurately to the correct mental impulses set in motion by the sight of the letters to be typed, or even the thought of a word or words to be typed. The fact that the fingers move instinctively in correct order for the production of words or groups of words is due entirely to methodical practice.

The " Standard " Keyboard

The arrangement of the keyboard is known as the " Standard " or the " Universal," and it has now been adopted by the leading typewriter manufacturers. On " standard " keyboard machines the alphabetical letters are arranged in three rows in the following order:

Q W E R T Y U I O P
A S D F G H J K L
Z X C V B N M

In addition to these keys for the twenty-six letters of the alphabet, there are other keys for figures, fractions, commercial signs, and punctuation marks. Sometimes there is a slight variation in the arrangement of the keys for the miscellaneous characters, and also the actuating keys—shift lock, back spacer, etc. This standardisation of typewriters means that, with very little modification of the instructions, it is possible for a typist to operate any of the well-known machines.

The keyboard is divided approximately into two equal sections, one for each hand. Each section is sub-divided into a series of keys for each finger.

From " Sight " to " Touch "

Typists who are not conversant with the most modern method of keyboard operation will be well advised to make the change from " sight " to " touch," and they will find this book in every way suitable for its attainment. The " touch " method certainly calls for the exercise of greater learning effort, but it will be well repaid by conservation of energy and increased efficiency.

It may be necessary during the change-over for the typist to continue to type by sight, but there must be complete distinction between the visual work and the touch practice until the less competent method is eventually superseded. There should be a definite scheme of keyboard practice, and many "sight" typists who have had regular daily practice for thirty minutes over a reasonable period have been successful in their efforts to become "touch" typists.

Keyboard Diagrams

A diagram of the complete keyboard is essential for self-tuition, as it will help in memorising the keys during the early stages of instruction.

On p. 13 there is a diagram showing the division of the typewriter keyboard, with an indication of the sections allotted to the fingers of each hand. This diagram should be carefully studied from time to time during instruction, as it is in this way that the correct location of each key and its association with keys in other rows will be memorised. On some of the keys two characters or fractions are indicated, but, until instructions are given for the operation of the shift key and the shift lock, the top characters will not be typed. Machines differ and there is usually one blank key at the top which is the BACK SPACER. The long bar *above* the top row of keys is the Tabulator bar, although on some older machines there may not be a bar but another blank key, usually provided on the right-hand side (see p. 18). There may be minor differences, and most typewriter manufacturers will supply a chart of their own keyboard free of charge if they are asked to do so.

Many manufacturers will also supply, upon request, pamphlets describing the different parts of their particular make of machine, and most of them are very willing to answer postal queries, should the student still be

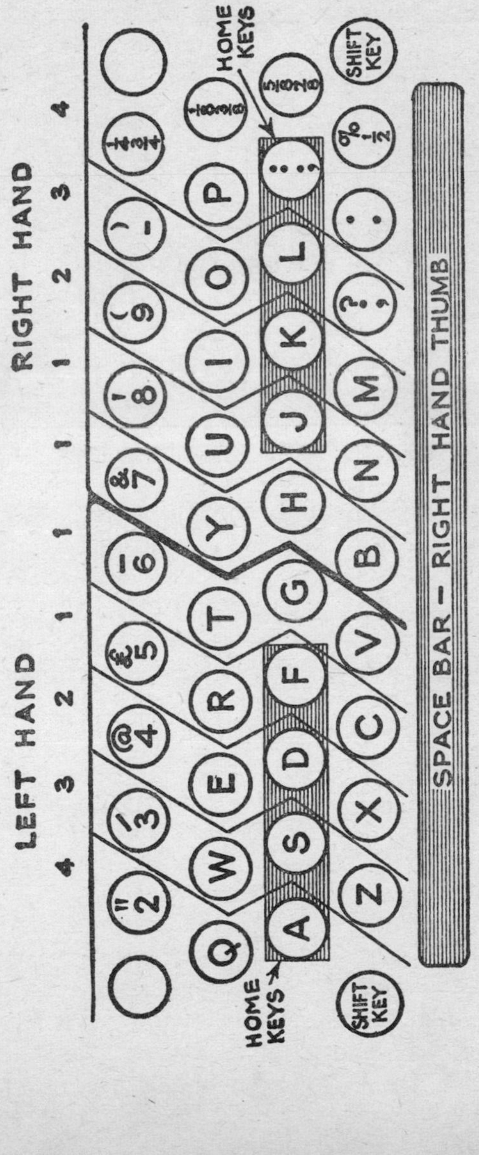

Division of Typewriter Keyboard.

in doubt about the function of any key on her typewriter.

In the sections dealing with keyboard mastery, diagrams are given at the head of the exercises, showing the particular part of the keyboard on which those exercises are mainly based.

SECTION II

PARTS OF THE TYPEWRITER— CARE OF THE TYPEWRITER

BEFORE keyboard instruction can begin, it is desirable to become acquainted with the most important parts of the typewriter. The details given below relate to those parts of the machine brought into use during the keyboard instruction. They will prove helpful to those not yet familiar with typewriters, and enable them to identify the various devices on their machines. The majority of the terms are self-explanatory, and the positions of the parts of the machine are easily ascertainable. The maker's handbook, which is always provided with a typewriter, should be read very carefully.

There are alternative terms (for example, *platen* for *cylinder*), and also slight variations in the construction of the various standard machines, but the supplementary information to be obtained from the instruction books issued by the typewriter companies will help towards a proper understanding of each individual part of the machine.

The arrangement of the details which follow is alphabetical, and not necessarily in order of operation. When reference is made in subsequent sections to parts of the typewriter, it will be well to refer to this section to understand the function of each part.

Back Spacer

When fully depressed this key moves the carriage back one space at a time. Where it is necessary to go back more than five spaces the carriage release lever may be used.

Bell, Warning

The bell rings about six spaces before the end of the line of writing.

Carriage

The whole of the mechanism that travels across the top of the machine. On each depression of a key or the space bar it moves one space from right to left. The carriage-frame contains the cylinder (or platen), paper feed rollers, and the line space mechanism.

Carriage Release Lever

This lever, on depression, throws out of action the escapement (a toothed rack) and enables quick and free movement of the carriage to the right or to the left.

Cylinder

The cylinder (or platen) is the large roller in the middle of the carriage, and it carries the paper in position.

Cylinder Knobs

Twirlers or hand-wheels fitted at each end of the cylinder; they are turned for the insertion and for the removal of the paper.

Line Space Gauge

This gauge is marked "1," "2," and "3," corresponding to three different line spaces, and the distance which the line space lever rotates the cylinder is determined by the setting of the gauge. There are six single-line spaces to the inch. On some typewriters, the line space gauge is marked for half-line spaces as well.

Line Space Lever

Used for turning up the paper when desired. At one operation the carriage is returned to the position set, and the paper is ready for the beginning of a new line. This lever is struck with the left hand flat (palm downwards), so that the first finger carrying out the operation has the support of the other fingers.

Margin Release

Depression of this key temporarily removes the set margin and permits the extension of the line of writing.

Margin Stops

Margins are regulated by the setting of the right-hand and left-hand margin stops at any desired position. These stops prevent movement of the carriage beyond a set point.

Paper Fingers

Adjustable paper clips or small rollers for holding the paper firmly in position.

Paper Gauge

This is an adjustable gauge, which ensures that the left-hand edge of the paper is always inserted into the machine at the same point.

Paper Release Lever

On depression of this lever the paper is free for proper adjustment or for removal from the machine.

Paper Scale

A gauge, marked or graduated, to coincide with the letter spaces; it indicates the length of the line of writing. There are ten letter spaces to the inch (Pica type) and twelve (Elite type).

Paper Table

The paper rests on this metal plate behind the cylinder while it is being fed through the rollers.

Ribbon Shift

There are three positions for this: (1) for using the top half of the ribbon; (2) for using the lower half of the ribbon; and (3) for disengaging the ribbon when a stencil is being cut.

Shift Keys

One on each side of the keyboard. They change the position of the mechanism so that the capitals or upper-case and miscellaneous characters can be typed.

Shift Lock

This temporarily locks the carriage for the continuous writing of capitals or upper-case and miscellaneous characters. By depression of a shift key the carriage resumes its normal position.

Space Bar

The long bar at the bottom of the keyboard. Each time it is depressed, the carriage moves one space. It should always be depressed by the right-hand thumb.

Tabulator Bar or Key

On full depression of this bar or key the carriage moves rapidly to points previously set for the preparation of tabular work.

Variable Line Spacer

A knob at the end of the cylinder which frees the line space ratchet and allows for any desired spacing between lines of typewritten matter.

CARE OF THE TYPEWRITER

A typewriter is an expensive machine, and the efficiency of the service it renders will depend largely on the care taken to keep it in good working order.

Removal

Damage is often due to lack of care when conveying the machine from one table to another. The hands should be placed under each side of the frame, so that they take the full weight, and the typewriter should be carried with the keys away from the body, so that there is no danger of their becoming bent. Never lift the machine by holding each end of the cylinder. Disregard of this instruction may result in serious damage to the machine.

Dust

The chief cause of trouble is dust, and any accumulation should be removed daily; this should be one of the first morning duties of the typist. When making an erasure, endeavour to prevent the dust from falling into the mechanism; move the carriage as far as possible to the left or to the right, according to the position of the erasure. Removal of the paper for the erasure and re-insertion in the machine for typing the correction is a more effective method. When not in use a cover should be placed on the machine.

Oiling

Oil should be applied to the typewriter regularly but sparingly. A good general rule is to oil points where friction occurs. A wire taper should be dipped into the oil-bottle and the lower end applied to the friction point. Wipe away any visible excess. On no account should oil be used on the typebars or in the segment in which the typebars move. Dust will adhere to oil and will cause the typebars to "stick". Use the best oil, and obtain it either from a typewriter company or from a firm marketing typewriting accessories.

Cleaning Type

The type may become clogged when a new ribbon is in use, and letters which need special attention are the "closed" letters such as o, e, a, d, b, g, p, q, etc. An effective way of removing the dirt is by the application of a little benzine on the type-faces. A type brush should be used, and the movement should be forward and backward, not across the type basket which contains the typebars. There are also various mechanical cleaners on the market, which can be bought from any office stationers.

Repairs

The question of repairs is seldom dealt with in typewriting manuals. It is possible for an experienced typist to make minor adjustments, but when a machine is manipulated with care there is usually little need for the services of the typewriter mechanic. If, however, any serious defect develops, do not interfere with the mechanism, but obtain the services of a skilled mechanic.

SECTION III

PRELIMINARIES TO KEYBOARD MASTERY

THE main parts of the machine have now been noted, but there are still some important matters to be considered before keyboard operation can begin.

Position at Machine

To carry out any machine work in an efficient manner it is generally agreed that a comfortable position will ensure complete command during operation, and the typewriter is no exception.

Furniture most suited for typewriting cannot always be secured, but an endeavour should be made to adjust the height of the table and chair so that it is possible to sit comfortably. Wooden blocks, footrests and cushions can be used for this purpose. The beginner should sit with the elbows near the sides of the body and the forearms parallel to the slope of the typewriter keyboard.

When the machine has been placed with the bottom edge of the frame approximately in line with the front of the table, the typist should adopt a natural and easy position before the machine, with the body inclined slightly forward. It is advisable to have an adjustable chair, fitted with a back-rest but without arms; otherwise the proper movement of the forearms will be impeded.

During the depression of the keys the backs of the hands should be kept perfectly level with the slope of the keyboard, and the fingers should be bent at the middle joint. There should be very little movement of the wrist.

The feet should rest firmly on the floor or on a footrest; their position should be varied occasionally, as slight movement will avoid strain or tension.

It is important that the typewriting table should be in a good light. Most typists prefer the copy to be on the right-hand side of the machine, and the table should, if possible, be placed in such a position that no shadow falls on the copy.

Paper Insertion and Removal

The method of inserting the paper is a simple operation, and can be performed rapidly. Place the paper to the left of the machine, with the length of the paper parallel to the front of the table. Then pick up the paper by putting the left hand with the palm and fingers spread on top and the thumb underneath. Lift the paper to the carriage of the machine with the thumb in front and the fingers behind until it rests lightly on the feed rolls—the small rollers between the paper table and the cylinder. Ensure that the left-hand edge of the paper is against the paper gauge at " o ". Then " swish " the paper into position with a quick turn of the right-hand cylinder knob. If the paper has not fed in evenly it can be adjusted by using the paper release lever.

Withdrawal of the paper should also be done rapidly. The paper should be held at the top left-hand corner between the thumb and first finger of the left hand and lightly pulled at the same time as the right-hand cylinder knob is quickly turned. Another method is to use the paper release lever and remove the paper quietly from the machine.

The Backing Sheet

An improvement in the appearance of the typewritten work will be secured by the use of a backing sheet—a sheet of stout paper placed behind the typewriting paper—particularly when only one sheet of paper is required in the machine. A backing sheet helps to preserve the even surface of the cylinder, and a mark on the backing sheet will indicate when the bottom of the paper is being approached.

Depression of Keys

Cultivate a light touch. Do not push or press the keys; tap them with a light, quick blow, and this will ensure a clear and sharp impression. After a little practice the operator will be able to judge the degree of pressure that is necessary to obtain the best result. The finger must leave the key immediately on depression, so that the typebar is not restricted in its downward movement. Punctuation marks require a lighter touch than that used for the other keys. A heavy depression of the full stop, comma, and the hyphen is likely to puncture the paper.

Rhythm

For rhythmic work there must be absolute regularity of key depression—the equal timing of each stroke. Although the rate of operation may be slow, the interval between each depression should be equal. In order to gauge accurately the amount of time necessary, a little preliminary practice is advisable, with a watch with a second hand or with a metronome. Tap at one stroke a second on the table for, say, thirty seconds for an appreciation of what constitutes a speed of one stroke a second, and then increase the rate to two strokes a second. These are the speeds recommended for exercises in the keyboard mastery sections. An additional help is the gramophone. The playing of some even tempo tunes will convey the requisite rhythmic action. There is an evenness of beat in such music, and it is this equal interval between each stroke that is essential during typewriter keyboard training.

Type Sizes

The sizes of typewriter type in most general use are Pica and Elite. There are ten letters to the inch for Pica type. Elite type is a smaller type, and there are twelve letters to the inch. The exercises in the keyboard mastery sections are in Pica type. It will require a very elementary arithmetical calculation to ascertain the space required for a line containing a similar number of letters of Pica and Elite. A line of writing containing sixty characters of Pica type (or a space in lieu of a character) will occupy six inches, but the same number of characters in Elite type will take up only five inches.

Paper

International Paper Sizes A4 (8·3″ × 11·7″) and A5 (8·3″ × 5·8″) have now taken over from the standard quarto (8″ × 10″) and foolscap (8″ × 13″). The A4 and A5 should be used for practice to encourage the learner to prepare for "office style" typewriting. Good quality paper is always more economical as both sides can be used.

Personal Preferences

That typewriting should be done by "touch" is beyond dispute, but, apart from definite methods of operation, there are few hard-and-fast rules regarding the production of an ordinary piece of typescript. The general layout is therefore largely decided by personal preference, but throughout an individual piece of work there must be uniformity in such matters as indentation (the leaving of a space at the beginning of the first line of a paragraph) and spacing, after punctuation. A paragraph is normally indented five spaces from the left-hand margin. In the case of spacing after punctuation there are at least three recognised methods, but the one recommended in this book will suit admirably. If there are any particular " rules of the house " in which one is employed they must be carried out and one's own preferences disregarded.

SECTION IV

KEYBOARD MASTERY: (I) SECOND ROW

THE most important section of the typewriter keyboard will naturally receive first consideration. It consists of eight keys in the second row from the space bar, known as the " home keys," and from these keys the sense of location of the whole keyboard will be developed.

These home keys are a s d f for the fingers of the left hand and ; l k j for the fingers of the right hand. They are often referred to as the " guide keys," although it is generally considered that the guide keys are the two home keys operated by the little fingers—a and ;. The following diagram shows the arrangement of the home keys (the shaded sections), and should be very carefully examined:

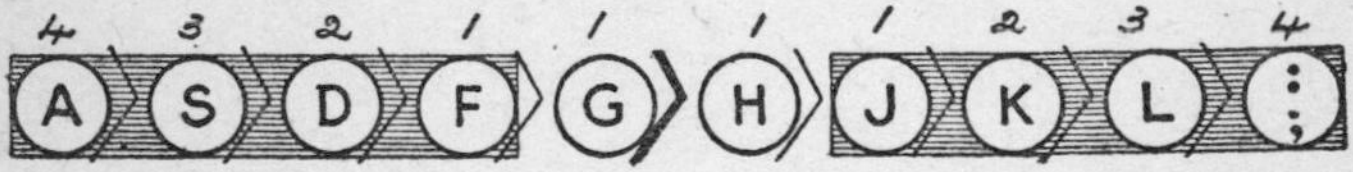

During keyboard operation the tips of the fingers indicated in the diagram should rest lightly (so lightly that there is no actual depression of the keys) on the home keys. The little finger of the left hand operates a and the third, second, and first fingers the remaining keys for the left section—s d f. The little finger of the right hand operates the semicolon (;), and the third, second, and first fingers the remaining keys for the right section—l k j.

Repeat aloud several times a s d f and ; l k j in this order, and during the repetition tap the respective fingers on the table at equal intervals of time—one tap a second—as mentioned under "Rhythm" on p. 23. This will give a distinct impression of the order of the home keys, and also the timing for each depression. With these points clearly in mind, the first stage of keyboard operation can begin.

Place a sheet of paper (with backing sheet) in the machine for the working of the first exercise; set the margin stops at 10 and 60, and return the carriage to the left-hand margin stop for the beginning of the first line. Set the line space gauge for double-line spacing.

Place your fingers on the home keys, as shown on the diagram opposite. Every time you remove your left hand from the keyboard to return the carriage at the end of a line, you must be able to return your left-hand fingers to their home keys *without looking at the keyboard.*

Before you start Exercise 1, practise placing your fingers on the home keys until you can do it quickly without looking.

Each key should be struck lightly and at equal intervals of time—one stroke a second for the first two exercises and two strokes a second for the remainder of this section. If, however, there is any difficulty in typing accurately at two strokes a second, revert to one stroke a second until repeated practice makes the increase possible. It is essential at this stage that there should be absolute accuracy and even depression; speed will come with regular practice.

Place the copy on the right-hand side of the typewriter. This will prevent the copy from being hidden by the left forearm when the carriage is returned.

EXERCISE I

1. asdfasdfasdfasdfasdfasdfasdfasdfasdfasdfasdf
2. ;lkj;lkj;lkj;lkj;lkj;lkj;lkj;lkj;lkj;lkj;lkj;lkj
3. asdfgfasdfgfasdfgfasdfgfasdfgfasdfgfasdfgfasdfgf
4. ;lkjhj;lkjhj;lkjhj;lkjhj;lkjhj;lkjhj;lkjhj;lkjhj
5. fdsa jkl; fdsa jkl; fdsa dfas kj;l dfas kj;l dfas
6. sfad lj;k sfad lj;k sfad sadf l;kj sadf l;kj sadf

EXERCISE 2

```
1.  as ad af ag ;l ;k ;j ;h as ad af ag ;l ;k ;j ;h
2.  ;l ;k ;j ;h as ad af ag ;l ;k ;j ;h as ad af ag
3.  as ;l ad ;k af ;j ag ;h as ;l ad ;k af ;j ag ;h
4.  sa l; da k; fa j; ga h; sa l; da k; fa j; ga h;
5.  sd df sd df lk kj lk kj sd df sd df lk kj lk kj
6.  gf fg gf fg jh hj jh hj gf fg gf fg jh hj jh hj
```

Reminders: set the margin stops at 10 and 60; adopt correct position at keyboard; do not look at the keyboard; fingers to rest lightly on home keys; equal intervals between each key depression; one stroke a second; the line numbers are for reference only.

Make sure that it is in such a position that you can read the exercises easily without having to alter your position at the machine.

The four keys memorised for the left hand (a s d f) are required for the first line of Exercise 1, and, with the eyes on the copy, this combination of letters is to be repeated twelve times. While the home keys for the left hand are being struck for this first line, the fingers of the right hand should be resting lightly on their respective home keys. The line numbers are inserted for reference only, and the reminders given with the exercises should be carefully noted before proceeding to type.

When the end of each line is reached, the carriage should be returned to the right of the machine by contacting the carriage release lever with the side of the first finger of the left hand (palm downwards), and this finger should be supported by the other fingers of this hand. If this lever is struck smartly the double action of turning up the paper for the next line and returning the carriage to the left-hand margin stop will be accomplished.

During the return of the carriage the right hand keeps its home key position and the left hand returns to the home keys immediately on completion of the carriage return movement.

Now note the second line. This deals with the four keys memorised for the right hand (; l k j), and completes the eight home keys. The fingers of the left hand should be in the normal home key position during the typing of the second line.

In the third and fourth lines the additional keys (g and h) are introduced; they are shown in the diagram at the head of the exercises. The first finger of the left hand will move slightly to the right from f to g, and the first finger of the right hand will move slightly to the left from j to h. The other fingers should not be moved when the additional key is struck. Immediately after the depression of g or h the finger should return to its home key. Each series of letters in these lines finishes on the home keys for the first fingers—f and j.

For the fifth and sixth lines the order has been varied. Repeated practice will ensure that as each letter is read the appropriate finger will respond to the direction by the brain and depress the key for the letter shown in the copy.

A space is required after each series of letters in the fifth and sixth lines, and the space bar should always be struck with the right-hand thumb, but the fingers should not leave the home key positions. The time taken for the depression of the space bar should be equal to that for a letter or character key; in this way correct rhythm will be maintained.

At the first attempt there is no need to type an exercise line for line—the numbers are inserted for reference only. Each line in the exercises should be treated as a separate item and copied several times. For repetition practice, type in single-line spacing. After the repeated practice on each line, type in double-line spacing at least one accurate copy of the whole exercise.

More work with the space bar is given in Exercise 2, and Exercises 3 and 4 consist of words built up from the home keys and the additional keys for the first finger of each hand.

EXERCISE 3

1. sad; lag; sad; lag; sad; lag; sad; lag; sad; lag;
2. jag; has; jag; has; jag; has; jag; has; jag; has;
3. fad; ask; fad; ask; fad; ask; fad; ask; fad; ask;
4. lad; aha; lad; aha; lad; aha; lad; aha; lad; aha;
5. gas; ash; gas; ash; gas; ash; gas; ash; gas; ash;
6. had; sag; had; sag; had; sag; had; sag; had; sag;

EXERCISE 4

```
1. dash; half; dash; half; dash; half; dash; half;
2. lass; glad; lass; glad; lass; glad; lass; glad;
3. gall; shag; gall; shag; gall; shag; gall; shag;
4. flask shall flask shall flask shall flask shall
5. salad glass salad glass salad glass salad glass
6. galas flags galas flags galas flags galas flags
```

Reminders: *set margin stops at* 10 *and* 60; *increase speed to two strokes a second; right-hand thumb for space bar depression; first finger returns to home key after striking additional key; little movement of the wrists; ensure equal interval between each stroke.*

On the completion of each exercise examine the work and encircle all mistakes in pencil. Find out the cause of these errors—uneven key depression, wrong fingering, etc.—and then type the corrections several times. If any of the typed letters be " shadowed " it is assumed that the keys are being *pressed*, instead of tapped with a staccato movement.

Finally, remember that this first section of keyboard mastery is of special importance; it is with this second row of keys that the remainder of the keyboard is associated, and extended practice on the exercises will be well worth the time spent in this way.

SECTION V

KEYBOARD MASTERY: (2) THIRD ROW

When the ten keys dealt with in the previous section have been memorised and accurate copies of the first four exercises have been completed, attention can be directed to the subject of this section—the third row of keys.

Apart from the question of accuracy, the typewritten work should be examined from the point of view of evenness of touch. There should not be varying shades of thickness; each letter should have the appearance of having had the same intensity of depression. If some fingers appear to be weak (and very often this is the case with the little fingers), there should be additional practice with the letters that show any such weakness.

The third row includes ten additional letters of the alphabet, five for the fingers of each hand. The order in which they appear is shown in the following diagram:

When the correct position at the machine has been taken up, and the fingers have been placed on the home keys, the keys of the third row can be operated and memorised. They are in a position above and slightly to the left of their corresponding keys in the second row. An examination of the keyboard diagram on p. 13 or the diagram at the head of the exercises in this section will show the direction of the movement required.

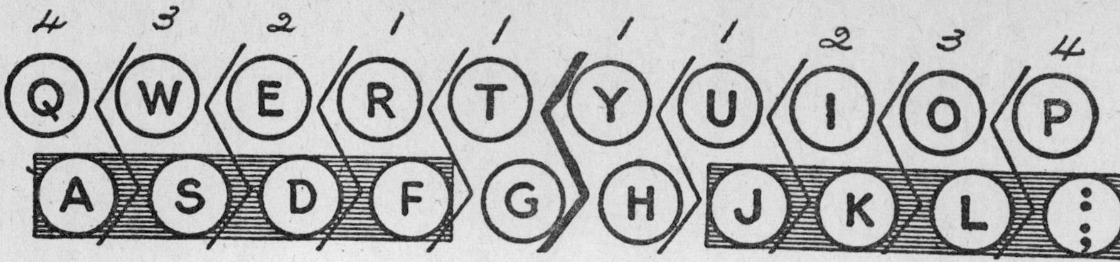

EXERCISE 5

1. aqa ;p; aqa ;p; aqa ;p; aqa ;p; aqa ;p; aqa ;p;
2. sws lol sws lol sws lol sws lol sws lol sws lol
3. ded kik ded kik ded kik ded kik ded kik ded kik
4. frf juj frf juj frf juj frf juj frf juj frf juj
5. fgt jhy fgt jhy fgt jhy fgt jhy fgt jhy fgt jhy
6. gtg hyh gtg hyh gtg hyh gtg hyh gtg hyh gtg hyh

EXERCISE 6

```
1. aqw ;po aqw ;po aqw ;po aqw ;po aqw ;po aqw ;po
2. swe loi swe loi swe loi swe loi swe loi swe loi
3. der kiu der kiu der kiu der kiu der kiu der kiu
4. frt juy frt juy frt juy frt juy frt juy frt juy
5. gtr hyu gtr hyu gtr hyu gtr hyu gtr hyu gtr hyu
6. qaw p;o wse oli edr iku qaw p;o wse oli edr iku
```

Reminders: set margin stops at 10 and 60; find home keys position without looking at the keyboard; the touch should be as light as possible; time for depression of space bar the same as for character key; examine work, encircle all errors, and type corrections several times.

In order to associate correctly the keys of the second and third rows the first practice will be to reach from the home keys to the third row. With the little finger of the left hand strike the guide key a. With the same finger reach upward and slightly to the left to strike the q key, and then return the finger to the second row and again strike the key for a. The movements should be repeated several times, with a space between each series of letters, as:

aqa aqa aqa aqa aqa aqa aqa aqa

A similar movement will then be made by the third, second, and first fingers for this association of keys for the left hand, as:

sws sws sws sws sws sws sws sws
ded ded ded ded ded ded ded ded
frf frf frf frf frf frf frf frf

When the key in the third row is being struck, only the operating finger should move upward, the remainder keeping their home key positions. This movement is a little difficult at first, but, with the hands extended and the finger-tips resting lightly on the table, the finger movements can be practised away from the keyboard.

In the second row the first finger of the left hand was allotted an additional key (g), and there is a corresponding key (t) in the third row for the same finger. Strike the home key f; then with an upward and slightly right movement strike the key for t. Practise this exercise several times, as:

fgt fgt fgt fgt fgt fgt fgt fgt

The four fingers of the right hand should have been on their respective home keys (; l k j) and ready for action. Strike with the little finger the key for the semicolon; then with an upward and slightly left movement strike the key for p, and return the finger to strike the guide key, as:

;p; ;p; ;p; ;p; ;p; ;p; ;p; ;p;

The same movements should then be followed in regard to the other home keys for this hand and the associated keys in the third row, as:

lol lol lol lol lol lol lol lol
kik kik kik kik kik kik kik kik
juj juj juj juj juj juj juj juj

The first finger of the right hand was called upon to operate an additional key (h) in the second row, and there is a corresponding key (y) in the third row for the same finger. Strike the home key j; then with an upward and slightly left movement strike y. The following exercise should be typed several times, with an intervening space, as:

jhy jhy jhy jhy jhy jhy jhy jhy

So far this preliminary practice has required the use of each hand separately. The disengaged hand should have remained in the home keys position, except, of course, for the return of the carriage.

Exercise 5 is based on the above directions, and the last two lines contain the additional keys for the first fingers. Instead of repeated practice on one series of letters, alternate use is made of each hand. This will give a balanced effect to the keyboard work.

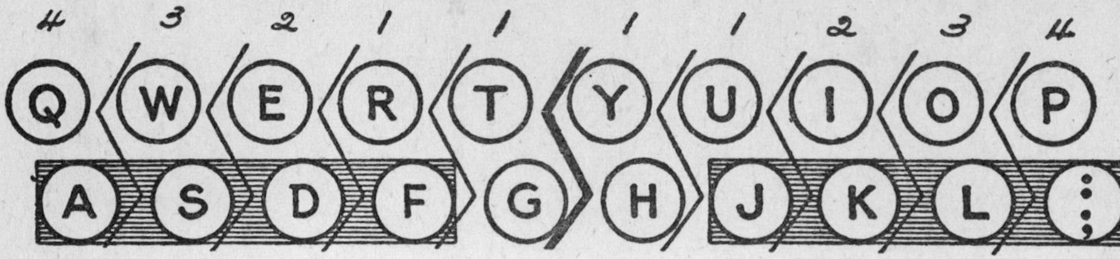

EXERCISE 7

1. dear poll feat jill gear oily tear holy read hill
2. hoop star hull deaf loop dare pulp gate pill fret
3. lap fit hay pay dog key for hey fur jay foe; fig;
4. flay dial work goal fury girl dual dish fowl quay
5. spelt prowl shape lapel shale palsy queue; furls;
6. ladder dapper fitter sallow ferret dagger gossip;

EXERCISE 8

```
1. they are sure that they were right at that period
2. at their request the first few words were deleted
3. there is a good supply of hot water at this hotel
4. goods like those are sure to get you the top rate
5. he helped us to pass the press proofs of the list
6. the guard said that the lads had paid their fares
```

Reminders: set margin stops at 10 and 60; hand not typing should remain in home key position; type at two strokes a second; timing of double letters should be even; examine work for accuracy and evenness of touch.

In Exercise 6 the series of letters in the first five lines begin in the second row and finish in the third row. The finger should return to the second row as each series is completed. In the sixth line each series begins and ends on the third row of keys.

Exercise 7 consists of words formed from letters in the second and third rows, and in the first two lines the words require alternate use of each hand. In the third, fourth, and fifth lines alternate use is made of letters in the right and left sections of the keyboard. This exercise ends with a selection of words with double letters. There is a tendency to increase the rate of operation when this occurs; the double letters should be typed with the same regularity as keys for different letters.

Short sentences in Exercise 8 complete the section, but the capital letter and period ordinarily required will be introduced at a later stage.

SECTION VI

KEYBOARD MASTERY: (3) FIRST ROW

WITH the ability at this stage to type words and sentences there will be a natural feeling of progress. If the exercises have been typed accurately and rhythmically, that feeling will be well justified, and the remaining letters of the alphabet can now receive attention. These letters are in the first row of the keyboard (just above the space bar), and they appear in the following order:

This row is usually considered a little more difficult than the second and third rows, because of the downward movement from the home keys. The first row will be memorised by its association with the home keys, and the movement necessary should be practised several times. The little finger of the left hand has no letter or character key in this first row, but it is given the work of operating the shift key. This key is used for securing capitals and miscellaneous characters, and will be fully explained in a later section.

To reach in the first row the keys associated with the home keys, the movement is downward and slightly to the left.

After finding the home keys without looking at the keyboard, strike the guide key a; then depress fully the shift key with the little finger and release it. The time taken for the depression of the shift key should

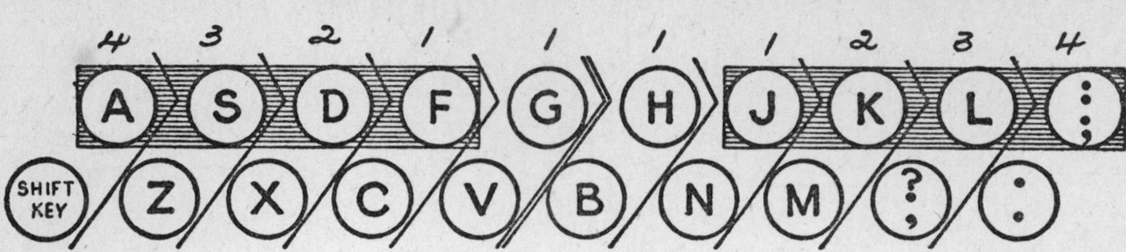

EXERCISE 9

```
1.  a*a ;.; a*a ;.; a*a ;.; a*a ;.; a*a ;.; a*a ;.;
2.  szs l,l szs l,l szs l,l szs l,l szs l,l szs l,l
3.  dxd kmk dxd kmk dxd kmk dxd kmk dxd kmk dxd kmk
4.  fcf jnj fcf jnj fcf jnj fcf jnj fcf jnj fcf jnj
5.  gvg hbh gvg hbh gvg hbh gvg hbh gvg hbh gvg hbh
6.  zxz ,m, cvc nbn zxz ,m, cvc nbn zxz ,m, cvc nbn
```

EXERCISE 10

```
1. asz ;l, asz ;l, asz ;l, asz ;l, asz ;l, asz ;l,
2. sdx lkm sdx lkm sdx lkm sdx lkm sdx lkm sdx lkm
3. dfc kjn dfc kjn dfc kjn dfc kjn dfc kjn dfc kjn
4. fgv jhb fgv jhb fgv jhb fgv jhb fgv jhb fgv jhb
5. aqz ;p. swz lo, dex kim frc jun gtv hyb aqz ;p.
6. zqz .p. zwz ,o, xex mim crc nun vtv byb zqz .p.
```

Reminders: set margins at 10 and 60; eyes on copy; note downward movement from second row; full depression of shift key in the same time as that taken for character key; type at two strokes a second.

be the same as for a character key. Accurate timing of the stroke for the shift key will be secured with repeated practice. After this shift key operation the little finger returns to strike the guide key a. The shift key depression does not move the carriage one space, and the typewritten work for this action will be a repetition of the guide key a. Count *one—two—three* while carrying out the movement.

Now with the third finger strike s; lower to strike z, and then return to strike s. Repeat these movements accurately several times, with a space between each series, and the line will appear as:

szs szs szs szs szs szs szs szs

Similar movements by the second and first fingers from the other home keys for this hand will give:

dxd dxd dxd dxd dxd dxd dxd dxd
fcf fcf fcf fcf fcf fcf fcf fcf

There is an additional key for the first finger; it is that for v, and its home key in the second row is f. Remember to return your finger to this home key after striking each letter:

gvg gvg gvg gvg gvg gvg gvg gvg

This completes the work for the left hand, and the practice will be continued for the right hand.

First, strike the semicolon, the guide key in the second row; then downward and to the left for the full stop, and back to the semicolon, as:

;.; ;.; ; ; ;.; ;.; ;.; ;.; ;.;

Continue this practice for the remaining home keys, as:

l,l l,l l,l l,l l,l l,l l,l l,l
kmk kmk kmk kmk kmk kmk kmk kmk
jnj jnj jnj jnj jnj jnj jnj jnj

The additional key in the first row for the first finger of the right hand is b, and its home key in the second row is j. Return your finger to this home key after striking each of the following letters:

hbh hbh hbh hbh hbh hbh hbh hbh

In the first five lines of Exercise 9 the series of letters already practised are given in alternate form. An asterisk in the first line indicates the depression of the shift key with the little finger of the left hand, but there will be no space movement for this depression. The sixth line deals only with characters in the first row.

For Exercise 10 the movements are varied, and each series in the first five lines ends with a key in the first row. The fingers will automatically return to the home key positions from the other rows, as each series begins with a key in the second row, but in the sixth line the reach is from the first row to the third row.

In the first two lines of Exercise 11 the words contain only letters from the first and second rows. In the remaining lines letters from all three rows of the keyboard are included, and each word requires alternate use of the right and left sections of the keyboard.

The first five words in each line of Exercise 12 are typed on alternate sides of the keyboard and repeated. They provide another example of the disengaged hand remaining in the home keys position while the other hand is striking the keys.

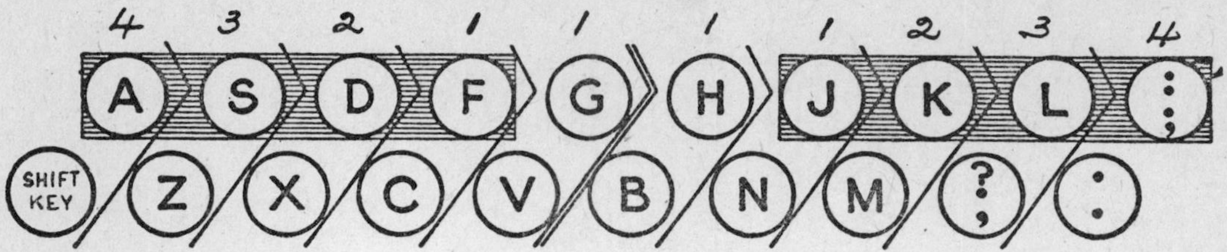

EXERCISE 11

1. cab ham van dab nag jam sac ban sax cad jab fan
2. and can mad lax bag jag bad nab cam lac dam man
3. amend label flame japan panel glebe brick snake
4. visor broth clays urban vodka angle lapel endow
5. chair mango docks neigh gland shame anent slant
6. spend penal chant handy smelt chaos bench cycle

EXERCISE 12

1. face limb raze boil axes face limb raze boil axes
2. card bulk aver lion fact card bulk aver lion fact
3. dace join cave kink arcs dace join cave kink arcs
4. gave plum tact bulb vast gave plum tact bulb vast
5. daze milk wave puny sect daze milk wave puny sect
6. save hymn cart inky aces save hymn cart inky aces

Reminders: set stops at 10 and 60; cultivate a light and even touch; do not look at the keyboard—eyes on the copy; examine typewritten work, encircle errors, and type correct words.

SECTION VII

KEYBOARD MASTERY: (4) TOP ROW

Up to this point the keyboard work has been connected with the twenty-six letters of the alphabet (not the capitals), and the punctuation marks for the semicolon, comma, and full stop.

This section will include the fourth (or top) row of keys, which, in the first place, introduces some arabic numerals (2 to 9), the hyphen, and a fraction. The remaining arabic numerals (1 and 0) are obtained by the small "l," and the cipher by the capital O. On some typewriters, separate keys for the figures "1" and "0" are included in the top row. In this case, the position of some of the keys may differ from the diagram given below, and if this should be so, the learner is recommended to make the appropriate alterations in the printed exercises. It will be seen in the following diagram of this row of keys that other

signs are given, but at the moment the work is concerned with the bottom portions only.

The first fingers of each hand will continue their dual task, and the four middle keys have to be operated by these two fingers.

Hitherto the reach from the home keys has been the width between one row, but for this top row a longer span is necessary. A glance at the diagram at the head of the exercises will show that, after leaving the third row, the movement from that row to the top is slightly to the right of the corresponding key in the third row. The movement necessary will be fully impressed on the mind by practice which combines the second row with the third and top rows.

Begin with the fingers resting lightly on the home keys. Strike the guide key a, then strike q, return the finger to a, and then move the finger upwards and slightly to the right, and strike 2.

aq2 aq2 aq2 aq2 aq2 aq2 aq2 aq2

Similar practice for the remaining home keys of the left hand and the corresponding keys of the third and top rows will give the following:

sw3 sw3 sw3 sw3 sw3 sw3 sw3 sw3
de4 de4 de4 de4 de4 de4 de4 de4
fr5 fr5 fr5 fr5 fr5 fr5 fr5 fr5

For the first finger the additional key is 6, and this should be typed with its associated keys in the other rows, as:

gt6 gt6 gt6 gt6 gt6 gt6 gt6 gt6

This completes the operation for the left hand, and the movements will be similar for the fingers of the right hand, which should have been in the home keys position during the typing of the previous lines.

Now for the right-hand practice, with the left hand in the home keys position. Strike the semicolon, the guide key for the right hand; reach upward and strike p, return the finger to its home key, and then reach upward and slightly to the right to strike ¾.

;p¾ ;p¾ ;p¾ ;p¾ ;p¾ ;p¾ ;p¾ ;p¾

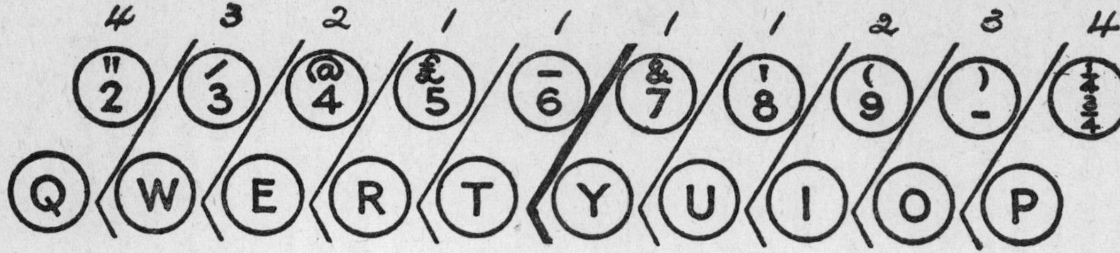

EXERCISE 13

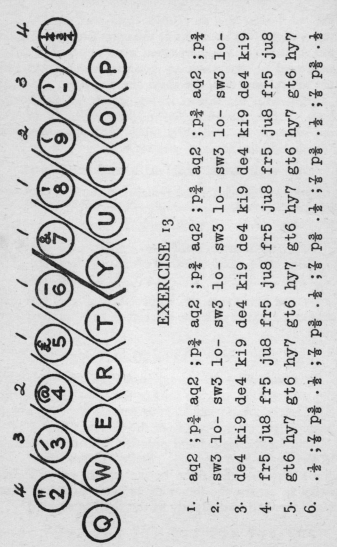

1. aq2 ;p¾ aq2 ;p¾ aq2 ;p¾ aq2 ;p¾ aq2 ;p¾ aq2 ;p¾
2. sw3 lo- sw3 lo- sw3 lo- sw3 lo- sw3 lo- sw3 lo-
3. de4 ki9 de4 ki9 de4 ki9 de4 ki9 de4 ki9 de4 ki9
4. fr5 ju8 fr5 ju8 fr5 ju8 fr5 ju8 fr5 ju8 fr5 ju8
5. gt6 hy7 gt6 hy7 gt6 hy7 gt6 hy7 gt6 hy7 gt6 hy7
6. .½ ;⅞ p⅜ .½ ;⅞ p⅜ .½ ;⅞ p⅜ .½ ;⅞ p⅜ .½ ;⅞ p⅜ .½

EXERCISE 14

1. a2a ;¾; a2a ;¾; a2a ;¾; a2a ;¾; a2a ;¾; a2a ;¾;
2. s3s l-l s3s l-l s3s l-l s3s l-l s3s l-l s3s l-l
3. d4d k9k d4d k9k d4d k9k d4d k9k d4d k9k d4d k9k
4. f5f j8j f5f j8j f5f j8j f5f j8j f5f j8j f5f j8j
5. g6g h7h g6g h7h g6g h7h g6g h7h g6g h7h g6g h7h
6. 23 24 25 26 27 28 29 2- 2¾ 34 45 56 67 78 89 9-

Reminders : set margin stops at 10 and 60 ; note movement from second row to the top row ; the letter 'l' is also used for the numeral " one " ; lighter depression of punctuation marks.

Follow this form of practice for the remaining home keys and their associated keys in the third and top rows, as:

```
lo- lo- lo- lo- lo- lo- lo- lo-
ki9 ki9 ki9 ki9 ki9 ki9 ki9 ki9
ju8 ju8 ju8 ju8 ju8 ju8 ju8 ju8
```

The additional key for the first finger is 7, and this is associated with h and y in the other rows, as:

```
hy7 hy7 hy7 hy7 hy7 hy7 hy7 hy7
```

The instruction up to this stage has dealt with thirty-nine of the forty-two keys, and the three remainings keys (fractions on the majority of machines) to be dealt with are operated by the little finger of the right hand. It will be remembered that in finding the home key position for the right hand, the little finger had to ignore for the time being the outside key. This is the fraction $\frac{7}{8}$ (on the right of the semi-colon). Its associated key in the third row is that for $\frac{3}{8}$ (on the right of p), and in the bottom row the fraction $\frac{1}{2}$ (on the right of the full stop).

The movements from and to the home keys row are similar to those already observed for the keys of the first three rows. Practise this series of fractions and the associated keys several times, with a space between each series, as:

;⅞; p⅜p .½. ;⅞; p⅜p .½. ;⅞; p⅜p .½.

For those who may have a weakness of the little fingers, this line and the first line in this section (aq2) will help in strengthening those fingers so that they secure the correct key depression.

In Exercise 13 the above movements have been embodied, but each series is arranged to give alternate work on the right and left sections of the keyboard. The last line gives additional practice on three of the fractions and other characters operated by the little finger of the right hand. For Exercise 14 the work is arranged so that the fingers reach from the second row to the top row and back to the second row. The sixth line deals only with the top row.

Further practice for this section is provided in Exercise 15, which contains three-letter words built up exclusively of letters contained in the third row, and also a series of three numerals from the top row. The same procedure is followed in Exercise 16, the difference being four-letter words and a series of four numerals.

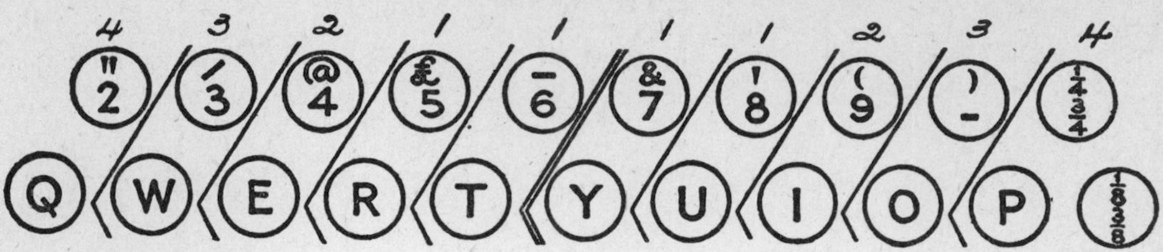

EXERCISE 15

1. tip 234 pit 456 try 789 wit 234 pry 456 yet 789
2. out 243 top 465 pet 798 ere 243 pro 465 tie 798
3. rye 244 pot 546 toe 879 pep 244 roe 546 pow 879
4. ewe 324 pop 564 eye 897 woe 324 yew 564 two 897
5. you 342 put 645 wet 978 pie 342 wry 645 pup 978
6. rut 344 tow 654 rue 987 ire 344 toy 654 pip 987

EXERCISE 16

1. tree 2345 weep 4567 peer 6789 quip 2345 prop 4567
2. peep 2435 weir 4576 tory 6798 wiry 2435 tyre 4576
3. type 2453 quit 4657 writ 6879 tyro 2453 wire 4657
4. your 3245 true 5674 wipe 7896 poor 3245 rite 5674
5. port 3254 trip 5746 tire 7968 pity 3254 troy 5746
6. rope 3452 wept 5764 pert 7986 tort 3452 tour 5764

Reminders: set margin stops at 10 and 60; all words contain letters in third row only; numerals in top row; keep eyes on copy during keyboard operation; encircle all errors and type corrections several times.

SECTION VIII

SHIFT KEYS AND SHIFT LOCK—COMBINATION SIGNS AND CHARACTERS

EACH of the forty-two character keys operate typebars on which are fitted two characters, and they may include a small (lower-case) and capital (upper-case) alphabetical character, a figure, a commercial sign, a punctuation mark, or a fraction. The keyboard diagram on p. 13 shows all the miscellaneous characters and signs on the top portion of the keys.

For these capital letters and miscellaneous characters the shift keys are necessary—they move the cylinder or the type segments for the correct type impression. There is a shift key on each side of the keyboard, usually at each end of the bottom row of keys. The shift keys are operated by the little fingers. If the character required is on the right-hand side of the keyboard, the left shift key must be depressed, and vice versa.

Careful practice is essential to secure correct depression of the shift key. It is different from that for the ordinary key depression, as the shift key is fully depressed and held down during the striking of the character key on the opposite side of the keyboard. The timing of this depression should be the same as for a character key, and ensure that there is no break in the rhythm. The finger should return to its normal home key position immediately the shift key is released.

The shift lock is depressed when several capital letters are to be typed in succession.

The first practice for shift key operation will deal with associated keys of the second, third, and fourth rows. The capitals (use of shift keys) are given for the second row; the lower-case letters for the third row, and the miscellaneous characters (use of shift keys) for the fourth row. The learner is reminded that on some machines, the keys may differ from those shown for the top row. The appropriate alterations should be made therefore.

Depress the right-hand shift key to its full extent, and use the little finger of the left hand to type A; release the shift key and then type the lower-case letter in the third row for the same finger q, and again depress the right-hand shift key to type the double quotation marks (") in the top row. Repeat these movements several times, as:

Aq" Aq" Aq" Aq" Aq" Aq" Aq" Aq"

Now combine the remaining keys for the left hand in the three rows under consideration, as:

Sw/ Sw/ Sw/ Sw/ Sw/ Sw/ Sw/ Sw/
De@ De@ De@ De@ De@ De@ De@ De@
Fr£ Fr£ Fr£ Fr£ Fr£ Fr£ Fr£ Fr£
Gt_ Gt_ Gt_ Gt_ Gt_ Gt_ Gt_ Gt_

Similar movements by the right hand and the depression of the left-hand shift key will complete the remaining five upper-case characters of the top row. Type five lines, as:

:p¼ :p¼ :p¼ :p¼ :p¼ :p¼ :p¼ :p¼
Lo) Lo) Lo) Lo) Lo) Lo) Lo) Lo)
Ki(Ki(Ki(Ki(Ki(Ki(Ki(Ki(
Ju' Ju' Ju' Ju' Ju' Ju' Ju' Ju'
Hy& Hy& Hy& Hy& Hy& Hy& Hy& Hy&

Fractions in the second, third and fourth rows should now be practised, with alternate use of the shift key and a space between each series, as:

$$\tfrac{5}{8}\tfrac{3}{8}\tfrac{1}{4}\ \ \tfrac{7}{8}\tfrac{1}{8}\tfrac{3}{4}\ \ \tfrac{5}{8}\tfrac{3}{8}\tfrac{1}{4}\ \ \tfrac{7}{8}\tfrac{1}{8}\tfrac{3}{4}\ \ \tfrac{5}{8}\tfrac{3}{8}\tfrac{1}{4}\ \ \tfrac{7}{8}\tfrac{1}{8}\tfrac{3}{4}\ \ \tfrac{5}{8}\tfrac{3}{8}\tfrac{1}{4}\ \ \tfrac{7}{8}\tfrac{1}{8}\tfrac{3}{4}$$

Other upper-case characters are contained in the three outside character keys of the bottom (or first) row; they are on the typebars already operated for the comma, full stop, and the $\frac{1}{2}$ fraction. With the comma on most machines is the question mark (or note of interrogation); the full stop appears twice on the one typebar and over the $\frac{1}{2}$ fraction there is the per cent sign %.

Depress the left-hand shift key to its full extent, and with the third finger strike the key for the bottom row (?); with the little finger strike the key to the right (the full stop) without shift key depression, and again depress the shift key while the little finger moves to the right to strike the key for the per cent sign, as:

?. % ?. % ?. % ?. % ?. % ?. % ?. % ?. %

Ordinarily it would not be necessary to release the shift key for the full stop, but the above combination is given for practice in the use of the shift key.

In Exercise 17 the first line deals with the practice work of this section, and the second line involves the operation of the same keys but using the shift key in a different order. The rate of operation for the first attempt should be one stroke a second, and afterwards two strokes a second. For the initial capitals in the third line the left-hand shift key will be required, and for the fourth line the right-hand shift key. In the fifth and sixth lines three-letter words are given alternately for the right and left sections of the keyboard.

Exercise 18 consists of words arranged for alternate use of the left and right shift keys.

All the alphabet letters, miscellaneous characters, fractions, and punctuation marks are included in Exercise 19, which provides excellent practice covering the whole of the keyboard. The shift lock will be used for the underscore in the third line.

Exercise 20 is arranged for shift lock practice, and the lock will have to be released for the typing of the dash (or hyphen) between the items in the list of subjects.

The top row containing arabic numerals and miscellaneous characters is not easy to memorise, and the diagram given at the head of the exercises in this section includes this row and shows its association with the third row.

Roman numerals

When roman numerals are required, they are compiled from the following letters—capital or small:

```
I  (1);      V   (5);      X  (10);
L (50);      C (100);      D (500);
             M (1,000)
```

Capitals are used for numbers with names of monarchs, chapters, or questions:

```
George VI  -  Chapter XX
      Question VII
```

Small letters are used for the numbering of paragraphs or subsections in Acts of Parliament, and for the numbers of the preliminary pages of printed books.

The following show a reference to a private Act of Parliament and also a page reference:

```
20 Geo. 5, c. xxix
     page vi
```

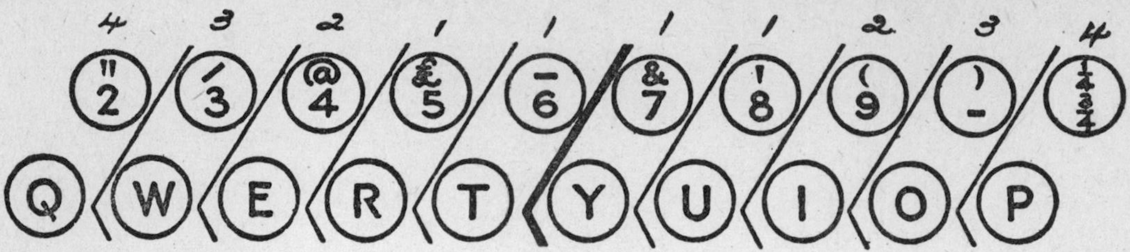

EXERCISE 17

1. Aq" :p¼ Sw/ Lo) De@ Ki(Fr£ Ju' Gt_ Hy& ⅝ ⅜ ¼ ?. %
2. aQ2 ;P¾ sW3 lO- dE4 kI9 fR5 jU8 gT6 hY7 ⅞ ⅛ ¾ ,. ½
3. Pr Ox La Ia Ka Me Us Ja Na Ye Ha Br Ur Ma He Mi
4. Qu Al Wh Sk Zo Ep Du Xe Cr Ri Fl To Gy Vo Ag Do
5. Ace Nun Cat Pun Tax You Fad Him Get Pin Car Nil
6. Sea Jim Wad Ink Vat Boy Gas Lop Wax Lip Arc Hop

EXERCISE 18

1. Area Lake Stab Kind Deaf John Face Hire Gain 23
2. Quad Pint Wait Omit Earl Idea Ream Unit Teak 45
3. Yank Zeal Male Xyst Nile Coke Back Vest Acts 67
4. Award Latin Stamp Knife Dance Joint Flour Heart
5. Brass Quart Pearl Watch Ocean Earth Index Ready
6. Uncle Total Young Cable Manor Vocal Naval Treat

Reminders: set the margin stops at 10 *and* 60*; little fingers to operate shift keys; shift key to be fully depressed and held during the striking of the character key.*

Roman numerals are not followed by a full stop, except at the end of a sentence.

A letter placed before one of greater value indicates that the first is deducted from the second to find the sum (XL = 40), and a letter placed after one of greater value indicates that both are added to find the sum (LX = 60).

A line placed over any symbol indicates that its value is multiplied by 1,000.

COMBINATION SIGNS AND CHARACTERS

When not on the keyboard, a number of signs can be made by the typing of one character with or over another.

Where two characters are required, one can be typed with or over another by holding down the space bar whilst the two characters are struck in succession, or by the use of the back spacer. For upper-case characters the space bar and shift key should be held down at the same time.

For some of these combination signs it will be necessary to use the variable line spacer to allow the characters to be slightly raised or lowered as required. It is not usual to raise the point above the line when typing decimals, except for advanced technical work.

For the plus sign it is recommended that pen and ink should be used, as the method sometimes followed (apostrophe over hyphen) is not very effective. This sign is included among the miscellaneous characters on some typewriter keyboards.

The combination signs and characters are arranged below in alphabetical order and should be typed several times.

Asterisk	⋇	small x and hyphen -
Caret	∠	solidus sign / and underscore _
Cedilla	ç	comma , under small c
Cent	¢	solidus sign / over small c
Dagger	I̶	capital I and hyphen -
Dash	-	hyphen - space before and after
Decimal point	3·5	full stop raised, or on line
Degrees	60°	small o raised after figure
Diaeresis	ä	double quotes " over letter
Division	÷	colon : and hyphen -
Dollar	$	capital S over solidus sign /
Equation	=	hyphen - and raised hyphen
Exclamation mark	!	apostrophe ' and full stop .
Feet	12'	apostrophe ' after figure
Fraction	6 1/16	solidus sign
Inches	9"	double quotes " after figure
Minus	121 - 3	hyphen - space before and after
Minutes	18'	apostrophe ' after figure
Multiplication	4 x 5	small x, with space before and after
Seconds	30"	double quotes " after figure
Section mark	§	small s over small s

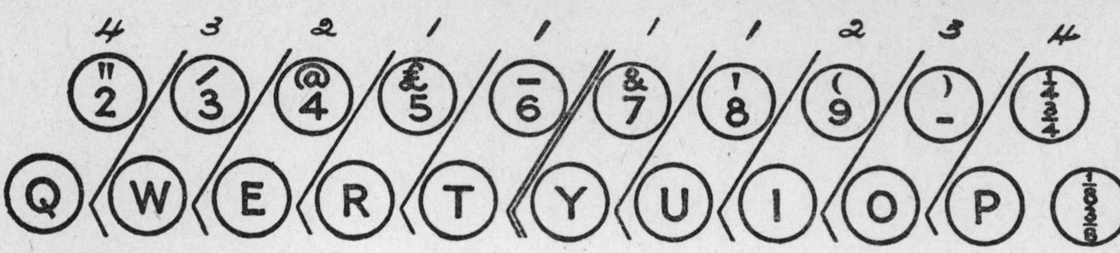

EXERCISE 19

1. Bizet & Co. offered us this page (6" x 8") for £9.
2. Today's quotations are $1\frac{1}{8}$, $2\frac{1}{4}$, $3\frac{3}{8}$, $4\frac{5}{8}$, $5\frac{3}{4}$ and $16\frac{7}{8}$.
3. Please send, <u>by return of post</u>, a cheque for £237.
4. Colon (:) and semicolon (;) appear on the one key.
5. Their invoice was for 5 copies @ 25p, less $12\frac{1}{2}$%.
6. Will John send them another copy of this 30p book?

EXERCISE 20

```
The following are among the "Teach Yourself" subjects:-
ASTRONOMY - BIOLOGY - CHEMISTRY - CARPENTRY - MECHANICS
PHYSICS - ELECTRICITY - EMBROIDERY - GEOLOGY - GEOMETRY
DRESSMAKING - GARDENING - MATHEMATICS - MUSIC - ALGEBRA
BUILDING - PHILOSOPHY - CALCULUS - MOTORING - ECONOMICS
TRIGONOMETRY - PHOTOGRAPHY - METEOROLOGY - SALESMANSHIP
```

Reminders : set stops at 10 *and* 60 *for Exercise* 19 *and at* 10 *and* 65 *for Exercise* 20 *; use shift lock for underscore in the third line ; shift lock to be used for five lines of Exercise* 20 *and to be released for hyphen between each item.*

SECTION IX

COPYING PRACTICE

THERE has been graded practice on all four rows of the machine with the object of attaining keyboard mastery, but a good deal of supplementary copying practice will be necessary to complete that mastery. The sense of location has by this time been fairly well developed, but regular daily copying practice will produce a noticeable improvement in accuracy and speed.

Even Margins

The setting of the stop for the left-hand margin ensures evenness throughout, but the same perfection cannot be secured for the right-hand margin of typewritten work. An examination of a printed page of this book will show that the printer can, by varying the space between words, guarantee an even right-hand margin, but on most machines the spacing between typewritten words is uniform. If it is necessary for the printer to divide a word at the end of the line, the division is indicated by using a hyphen.

Division of Words

In the earlier sections the exercises were arranged so that the right-hand margin finished at the same point of the scale, but in ordinary straightforward copying this uniformity cannot be obtained. Evenness can, however, be achieved to a reasonable extent by the use of the hyphen for the division of words, and it should be inserted only at the end of the line; it is incorrect to place a hyphen at the beginning of a line.

The general rules for the division of words may be summarised as:

(1) a word of one syllable should not be divided;
(2) a word should not be divided so that only two letters are carried forward to the next line;
(3) a hyphenated word should not be further divided;
(4) proper names should not be divided;
(5) dates should not be divided;
(6) series of numbers should not be divided;
(7) a person's initials should not be separated from his surname;
(8) a divided word should not end a page;
(9) a word should not be divided in such a way that the pronunciation of either half is affected;
(10) words containing double consonants may usually be divided between those consonants;
(11) sums of money should not be divided.

When the ringing of the bell gives warning of the approach of the end of the line of writing (usually six spaces), a quick decision has to be made regarding the division of the word, so that the rhythm of operation is not affected.

Line Spacing

Standard typewriters generally provide for three depths of spacing between lines—*single-line spacing* (no space between the lines); *double-line spacing* (a depth of one blank line between each line of typewriting); *treble-line spacing* (a depth of two line spaces between each line of typewriting). These three forms, in Pica typewriter type, are shown in Exercise 21, and when this is being typed the line space gauge should be properly adjusted for each depth of space and the line space lever operated to its fullest extent when the carriage is being returned to the right of the machine. The underscoring of the three items in the exercise will require the use of the shift lock. Here the underscore is used for emphasis, and other uses for it are referred to on p. 71.

Spacing after Punctuation Signs

The method of spacing recommended and adopted in the examples in this book is one space after a comma; two spaces after the full stop at the end of a sentence, and also two spaces after the exclamation mark, interrogation mark, colon, or semicolon. When the hyphen is used for the dash sign there should be a space both before and after the dash, and, when the quotation marks (or inverted commas) and parentheses (or brackets) are typed, they should not be separated by any space from the words which they enclose. Other methods of spacing are recognised, but, whichever style is decided upon, there must be consistency throughout the work. If, for example, three spaces are preferred after the full stop, this break should be made after every sentence in a typescript.

Copying Exercises

There is no need for the copying practice to be limited to the exercises given here. A section of any book or periodical can be used for this purpose, and it will be found that the leading article in the daily newspaper not only provides excellent typewriting practice, but also supplies a most informative survey of current affairs.

Practice material on one-line sentences is contained in Exercises 22 and 23, and each sentence should be copied separately several times. In this way a slightly increased speed in copying will be attained.

There are paragraphs of varying length in Exercises 24 to 30. In the first place, the exercise should not be taken as a whole, but each individual paragraph should be typed repeatedly until an increase in the speed is apparent. In order to obtain practice on the top row, figures and the miscellaneous characters are included in Exercise 31.

The names of the writers of the passages in Exercise 28 are shown in italic type, and in typewriting the underscore (which should be struck lightly) is used to indicate that the words underlined would in ordinary printed matter appear in italics. The underscore is also used for emphasising important words, for display work, for foreign words and phrases not anglicised, for scientific terms, and for authorities at the end of quotations or notes. This practice should be noted during the reading of books and periodicals.

When underscoring, the carriage should not be returned by means of the line space lever.

Where there is difficulty in typing any particular word, that word should be repeatedly typed until the letter combination can be copied at a fair rate of speed.

Do not be content with copying the complete exercises once only; they should be copied many times, even if one hundred per cent accuracy has been achieved at the first attempt. Repetition of any action facilitates its performance. On the first occasion it may be done indifferently, but at, say, the tenth attempt it will be performed with ease. An effort should be made to increase slightly the speed of operation at each successive attempt. And, here again, a previous direction is emphasised—*do not sacrifice accuracy to speed.*

EXERCISE 21

(Set margin stops at 20 and 55.)

Single-line spacing is generally used for long letters, invoices, tabular statements, poetry, plays, synopses, footnotes, lengthy documents. Usually double-line spacing is used between paragraphs to prevent a solid appearance.

Double-line spacing is used for short letters, lectures, literary work, essays, sermons, legal documents, and for copy intended for the printer.

Treble-line spacing is used for drafts, and for literary and legal work which may need revision.

EXERCISE 22

(Set margin stops at 10 and 65.)

```
To get satisfactory work clean your machines every day.
They have arranged to forward this book by parcel post.
See a specialist before you agree to another operation.
We have now seen a full account of the new competition.
If they miss this train they will have an hour to wait.
Type four letters on writing-paper and post them today.
They had another book dealing with short story writing.
He had gone before we were able to check the signature.
Many of the men were not able to work during last week.
Most people would agree with their view on the subject.
```

EXERCISE 23

(Set margin stops at 10 and 65.)

A perfect copy is possible when you are a touch typist.
I am pleased to acknowledge the good work done by them.
We are having another machine at the end of next month.
They have taken the house and will be moving in August.
I suggest an addition of one penny to the retail price.
Please co-operate with him as he is having a busy time.
If we add a form it will make a difference to the book.
There is now no doubt about the truth of their remarks.
It will be a pleasure for me to represent this company.
Please send him details of the "Teach Yourself" Series.

EXERCISE 24

An agenda is a list showing the order and nature of the business to be transacted at a meeting. Its preparation is usually entrusted to the secretary or to the person responsible for convening the meeting.

A folio is a sheet of paper folded once only so as to make two leaves. In book-keeping the word is used strictly to denote the two opposite pages of an account book numbered as one, but it now commonly means the same as a page.

Public companies are the joint-stock or limited liability companies which apply to the public for subscription, and which are composed of shareholders who are at liberty to sell their shares publicly without the consent of their fellow shareholders.

In general, a director is one who has the chief management of a scheme, design, or undertaking. More particularly, he is one of a number of persons chosen by a majority of the proprietors to conduct the affairs of some joint-stock undertaking.

In the case of a joint-stock company, the secretary is the officer who attends to all the legal requirements with regard to his company, and many Acts of Parliament impose personal responsibility on the secretary for the due compliance with certain provisions.

EXERCISE 25

Book-keeping is the art of keeping accounts, and recording in a regular, concise, and accurate manner the transactions of business men and others, so as to show the effect of the transactions upon the financial position of the parties.

The term " dividend " is applied either to the money which is divided amongst the creditors of a bankrupt out of his estate, or to the annual interest payable upon the National Debt and other public funds, and upon the shares in joint-stock companies.

An overdraft is the amount of cash which a banker allows his customer to draw out of his banking account in excess of the total moneys paid into the customer's account, and is generally secured by the deposit of some kind of security.

The objects of an audit are (a) the detection of errors of commission, (b) the detection of errors of principle, and (c) the detection of fraud. The auditor must see that the accounts truly represent the state of affairs of the concern.

The Bank of England was suggested by William Paterson, a Scotsman, and it received its charter of incorporation in the year 1694. It was constituted as a joint-stock company with a capital of £1,200,000, that sum being lent at interest to the Government of the day.

EXERCISE 26

An actuary is a person skilled in the calculation of the value of life annuities and insurances from mortality tables and upon mathematical principles, and in the preparation of reports, etc., in connection with insurance matters generally.

The Baltic Mercantile and Shipping Exchange (commonly known as "The Baltic") is an association of merchants, shipowners, brokers, and various allied trades connected with grain, oil, oil-seed, timber, coal, etc.

A bill of lading is an acknowledgment of the shipment of goods, which also contains the terms and conditions agreed upon as to their carriage. It is not necessarily the contract of carriage itself, though it is excellent evidence of it.

A legal day is the whole of the day, continuing up to midnight. When there is an obligation to do a certain thing by a fixed day, the whole day must pass before there can be default. For example, if rent is payable on a quarter day, it is not in arrear until the day following.

Shipbrokers are agents—persons or firms—in a seaport appointed by shipowners to carry out and perform all the necessary transactions connected with the business of their vessels whilst they are in harbour, such as entering and clearing the vessels, collecting freights, etc.

EXERCISE 27

Truth is always consistent with itself, and needs nothing to help it out. It is always near at hand, and sits upon our lips, and is ready to drop out before we are aware; whereas a lie is troublesome, and sets a man's invention upon the rack, and one trick needs a great many more to make it good.

Shirking duty, or running away from the things that we feel we ought to do, has a peculiarly demoralising effect on one's high purpose of right. Our judgment of what our duty is may be a mistaken one, but there is something imperious about the call of duty that makes the slighting of it a very serious matter indeed.

We shall never be sorry afterwards for thinking twice before we speak, for counting the cost before entering upon any new course, for sleeping over stings and injuries before saying or doing anything in answer, or for carefully considering any business scheme presented to us before putting money or name into it.

A public speaker is a mental guide. He leads his audience, step by step, through a succession of ideas, to a logical conclusion. If he is not prepared; if each of these steps or ideas is not clearly defined; if his thoughts are but vaguely conceived; if the bearing of the individual thoughts upon the conclusion is not clear, confusion follows.

EXERCISE 28

When a great man, who has engrossed our thoughts, our conjectures, our homage, dies, a gap seems suddenly left in the world; a wheel in the mechanism of our own being appears abruptly stilled; a portion of ourselves, and not our worst portion—for how many pure, high, generous sentiments it contains!—dies with him. —*Lord Lytton.*

It is idleness that creates impossibilities; and, where men care not to do a thing, they shelter themselves under a persuasion that it cannot be done. The shortest and the surest way to prove a work possible is strenuously to set about it. —*Robert South.*

The only freedom which deserves the name is that of pursuing our own good in our own way, so long as we do not attempt to deprive others of theirs, or impede their efforts to obtain it. Each is the proper guardian of his own health, whether bodily or mental and spiritual.—*John Stuart Mill.*

With malice toward none; with charity for all; with firmness in the right, as God gives us to see the right, let us strive on to finish the work we are in; to bind up the nation's wounds; to care for him who shall have borne the battle, and for his widow, and his orphan—to do all which may achieve and cherish a just and a lasting peace among ourselves, and with all nations.—*Abraham Lincoln.*

EXERCISE 29

Adequate filing in business will ensure the putting away of letters and other documents to preserve them from dirt and damage, and the arranging of them according to some plan, so that any letter or document can afterwards be obtained quickly. The plan to be followed must be worked out in sufficient detail to provide an exact place on the file for every letter or document used in business. Ease of reference is quite as important as preservation from damage.

Every caller at a business house is, as a member of the public, a potential buyer of goods or services, even if he has come to sell. His goodwill is valuable, no matter who he is, and its cultivation is in the hands of the receptionist. A naturally good receptionist is as rare as the naturally good hostess, and any girl who finds that, through shyness or inexperience, she is unequal to the occasion should learn the part of the receptionist as if it were a part in a play.

On the telephone the voice is an important factor and has to stand on its own merits, deprived of all assistance from gesture and facial expression. Many people who appear gracious and lucid in an ordinary conversation seem surly and confused on the telephone. All people using the telephone in business should study the faults they encounter at the other end of the line and strive to eliminate all of them at their end.

EXERCISE 30

For the folding of a large number of letters, statements, leaflets, etc., a folding machine is available. The papers are laid in packets on the feeding ledge of the machine, which is electrically driven and automatically fed, and folding proceeds at the rate of approximately 6,000 an hour. Many sizes of folds may be arranged for by adjusting the machine.

Correspondence is of the utmost importance in commercial life; and the letters and documents used in carrying out business should be carefully preserved, because they frequently form the record of a whole transaction, and very large sums of money may depend upon their careful preservation. All contracts should be committed to writing, accurately and clearly, so as to leave no room for dispute, and the documents should be so arranged and kept that they can be found with little delay whenever it is necessary to make subsequent reference to them.

You will learn much of your spelling by keeping your eyes open as you go along the streets, and by careful observation when reading your books or newspapers. There are also many attractive advertisements and posters which will help in teaching you how to spell. Whenever you see a word, the spelling of which causes difficulty, look closely at it to obtain a correct mental picture. This method is more valuable than trying to remember a number of spelling rules and their exceptions.

EXERCISE 31

The interrogation mark (?) is used when a direct question is asked; an example is: What is the price of Jack's book on Zoology?

The signs " & " (*and*), " @ " (*at*), and " % " (*per cent*) should not be used in the body of a document as a substitute for the word or words. The symbol " % " should not be used unless a number immediately precedes it.

The keyboard of a standard machine is usually fitted with the following fractions: ¼, ½, ¾, ⅛, ⅜, ⅝, ⅞, which are in most cases found sufficient for commercial work. One method of indicating fractions not on the keyboard is to use the shilling sign (or solidus), as: 5 1/16, 10 1/3, and 12 1/5.

The share capital issued remains at £6,000,000, and debenture stock is also unchanged at £1,750,000. With the reserves invested in the business the total capital employed in the business is £8,364,696. Creditors, £5,841, show an increase of some £1,800, and advances from the subsidiary companies, £310,000, compares with £248,000. The general reserve is increased by £70,000 transferred from revenue account, making a total at general reserve of £460,000.

SECTION X

DIFFICULT SPELLINGS

Correct spelling is of great importance in written English and needs little teaching to those who read much. Most of the users of this handbook will be book-minded people, and whether their reading includes modern thrillers, the classics, magazines, or the morning and evening newspapers, the unusual word should not be lightly passed. The constant copying of troublesome words in sentences will enable the typist to build up a sound knowledge of words. Those that give a great deal of trouble are the words ending in *-ible* and *-able* and double consonants—e.g., *embarrassed* and *harassed.*

Simple language is advisable, but it so often happens that it is the simple words about which there is doubt. One has only to consider *seize*, *accommodate*, *gauge* (often confused with the termination in *language*).

A selected list of difficult spellings is given in this section, and they are set out in two-column form. It is recommended that each page of the list should be typed in single spacing. In this way the correct spelling will be impressed on the mind. The meaning of the words is equally important, and a dictionary should be consulted when there is any doubt.

Never fail to consult an English Dictionary when there is uncertainty about the correct spelling of any word. Most people have recourse to a dictionary during their training and afterwards, and those who fail to do so generally give evidence of this lack of consultation by the spelling errors that are to be found in their typewritten work.

abhor
abhorred
abolish
abscess
accede
accept
accommodation
accumulated
achieving
aching
acquiesce
acquire
adherence
adjournment
admissible
adolescent
advantageous
advertise
aerial
affect
affreightment
aggregate
aggrieved
aghast
agreeable
aisle
alias
allege
allegiance
alliance
allotment
all right
altruistic
aluminium
amateur
ambiguity
ameliorate
amicable
ampersand
analogous
analyse
analysis
anomalous
appal
appalling
appendix
appropriate
appurtenances
argument
arthritis
ascend
asphalt
assassin
asset
assuage
asterisk
asthma
atrocious
attrition
augmentative

auspicious
authenticity
auxiliary
avoirdupois

bailee
bailor
bankruptcy
banquet
bareheaded
battalion
bazaar
beguile
beleaguer
believable
belligerent
beneficiaries
benefited
benign
bevel
bevelled
bias
bigoted
bilateral
biography
bluish
bona fide
book-keeping
boycott
bravado
brilliance
brittle
brunette

budgeting
buoy
bureaucracy
burlesque
by-election
by-law
by-product

cadaverous
cafeteria
calamitous
calligraphy
camaraderie
camouflage
canister
cantankerous
caprice
career
carriage
casualty
catalogue
catarrh
catastrophe
cedilla
ceiling
changeable
chaotic
chargeable
chauffeur
chiropodist
chronological
chrysanthemum
coalescence

coefficient
cognizant
coinciding
collateral
colleague
colloquial
collusion
combustible
commissionaire
commitment
committal
commodious
compatibility
comprehensible
compulsory
conceivable
conglomerate
connoisseur
conscientious
conspicuous
consummate
contentious
continent
controversy
conversazione
conversion
corduroy
corollary
corroborate
corruptible
counterfeit
credible
crucial
cul-de-sac
curriculum

damageable
debacle
debarred
debonair
debutante
decadence
decimate
decreeing
deducible
defeasance
defeasible
defensible
deferred
deficiency
deleterious
demarcation
deprecate
depreciate
descendant
desiccated
destructible
deterioration
deterrent
develop
development
dialling
diaphragm
dilemma
diminution
diphtheria

diphthong
discernible
discretionary
disparage
dispossess
dissatisfaction
disseminate
disservice
dissuasive
dubitable
dynamic

earnest
eavesdrop
ecclesiastical
ecstasy
edible
effervesce
efficacious
egregious
eligible
elucidate
embarrass
enamelled
encumbrance
encyclopaedia
ensemble
entrepreneur
epitome
equanimity
equidistant
equivalent
erstwhile
espionage
et cetera
etiquette
eucalyptus
evaporate
exacerbate
exchangeable
excusable
exhilaration
exorbitant
exorcize
extemporaneous
extraneous
exuberance
eyeing
eyewitness

facial
facile
fallacious
farinaceous
fatigue
fatiguing
feasible
felicitous
fictitious
flamboyant
floatation
focus
folio
fortuitous
freeing
frontispiece

fulfil
fulfilment

gaiety
garrulous
gaseous
gauging
gazetteer
glossary
gramophone
gratuitous
guarantor
guillotine
gullible
gusseted
gymnasium

half-caste
hallucination
haphazard
harass
harum-scarum
hazardous
herbaceous
heterogeneous
holocaust
hors-d'oeuvre
hullabaloo
humorist
humour
hygiene
hypothesis
hysteria

iconoclast
idiosyncrasy
illiteracy
illusion
immovable
impromptu
inaccessible
inadmissible
incognito
incombustible
incurred
indictment
indiscreet
infinitesimal
ingenious
insatiable
install
instalment
interim
irreducible
irresistible
isosceles

janitor
japanned
jargon
jay-walker
jeopardize
jetsam
jewellery
judiciary
judicious
juxtaposition

kaleidoscopic
kerosene
kilogram
kilowatt
kleptomania
knapsack
kudos

labelled
laborious
lackadaisical
laudatory
legion
liaison
libellous
litigation
logogram
loquacious
lovable
luscious

magnanimous
magnate
magnetize
maintenance
maisonnette
maladjustment
malfeasance
malignant
malingerer
malleable
malpractice
manageable
mannequin
manoeuvre
mantelpiece
marshalled
massacre
mayonnaise
medallion
mendacious
misapprehend
mischievous
mis-statement
mnemonic
monetary
multitudinous
mystery
mysticism

naïve
nauseate
necessitous
neurasthenia
nomenclature
nondescript
nonplussed
noticeable
nowadays
nullify

obeisance
obituary
obsession
occur
occurrence

odoriferous
officious
omissions
omitted
omniscience
onerous
ophthalmic
orthography
oscillations
ostentatious
outrageous
overmantel
overrate

palliative
panelled
paraffin
parallel
paralleled
paraphernalia
parcelled
pecuniary
penultimate
perceivable
perceptible
peregrination
peremptory
permeable
permissible
pernicious
persecute
perspicacious
perspicacity
persuasible
pertinacity
pessimism
pettifogging
pharmaceutical
phenomenal
picnicking
pigeon-hole
plagiarize
plenipotentiary
pneumatic
postcard
posthumous
potpourri
predecessor
predilection
proffer
pronounceable
pronunciation
propitious
pseudonym
psychology
purchasable

quandary
quantitative
quarrelled
querulous
queue
quinquennial
quintessence

raconteur

rapacious
rateable
readdress
rearrange
receivable
reciprocate
reconnaissance
recrudescence
recurrence
reminiscences
remissible
removable
rendezvous
reprehensible
rescind
rescission
résumé
reversible
rhapsody
rhythm
rivalled
riveted
rucksack
rudimentary

sacrilege
sacrilegious
sagacious
scepticism
scrutineer
secession
secretariat
sedentary
segregate
seizable
sententious
shoeing
silhouette
simultaneously
ski-ing
smithereens
soliloquy
sophisticated
sou'wester
sovereignty
spoliation
spontaneous
statistician
stencilled
stereotyped
stoicism
subsidiary
succinct
suggestible
suing
supercilious
supersede
surreptitious
susceptible
synonymous
synthesis

tactician
tautology
tawdry
teetotaller

tinge
tingeing
tiptoeing
titivate
towelling
trade-mark
trafficker
transferable
transferred
transmissible
trellised
tunnelled
tyrannical

ubiquitous
umbrageous
unanimous
unilateral
unkempt
unparalleled
unveiled
utilitarianism

valedictory
vapour
vaporize
vehicular
verdigris
verisimilitude
veterinary
vicarious
vicissitude
vigorous
vigour
voracious

wagon
wheelwright
wilful
wiseacre
witticism
woebegone
woollen
worsted

xylonite
xylophone

yardstick

zenith
zigzagging
zoology

SECTION XI

DECIPHERING MANUSCRIPT—PRINTERS' CORRECTIONS

So far the copying practice has been from typewritten examples or printed matter, but the majority of typists require the ability to decipher manuscript. This applies particularly to those engaged in copying and legal offices, as they may be called upon to produce fair copies from rough drafts written in almost illegible handwriting.

Before proceeding to prepare a typescript from a handwritten original the typist should read a fairly lengthy section, in order to become acquainted with the style of the writer. When there is any difficulty in deciphering a word, leave a space for the later insertion of the correct word, as it is possible that further acquaintance with the handwriting or the context will assist in the subsequent transcription of the word omitted.

Abbreviations

Abbreviations may be used, and for those employed in legal offices special lists are to be found in books dealing exclusively with this class of work. Some examples of longhand and legal abbreviations are included in the list of abbreviations at the end of this handbook. The following terminations may also prove useful:—

Word	*Abbreviation as in*
ary *as* y	reactiony
ever *as* vr	howvr

Word	*Abbreviation as in*
ial *as* l	substantl
ual *as* l	individl
ion *as* n	positn
ional *as* nl	professnl
ing *as* g	breakg
ings *as* gs	proceedgs
ment *as* mt	punishmt
fully *as* fly	wonderfly
ought *as* ot	brot, thot

The drafts are generally typed in double-line spacing, although treble-line spacing is the usual practice for legal documents, which often undergo drastic revision by each party before being prepared for signature. All abbreviations should be typed in full in the final copy.

Printers' Corrections

Exercises in this section are a test in reading straightforward but varied styles of handwriting, but handwritten drafts are not always so uniformly produced. Very often typists will be called upon to prepare typescripts from rough drafts containing marginal notes and interlineations, and they will need to know the instructional notes connected with the correction of printers' proofs. Many of the most common signs are given in the table on p. 108 and they are embodied in the corrected Exercise 37, of which a correct copy should be made.

The exercises on pp. 96 to 107 should be typed accurately, and on completion each copy should be carefully compared with its original—an important point often overlooked by typists.

EXERCISE 32

The question as to the original home of the tea plant is by no means settled, the point at issue being whether, after all, the true home of the plant is in the country naturally associated with it, viz. China, or in the neighbouring Indian province of Assam. The evidence in support of the latter contention is largely based upon the fact that the tea plant attains extraordinary luxuriance in Assam, greater, it is said, than that attained in any part of the Celestial Kingdom, and arguing that in its natural home a plant reaches its greatest development, supporters of this view maintain that it is in Assam and not in China that we are to look for the home of tea. It by no means follows, however, that the reasoning of this argument is sound, for it has been repeatedly noticed that plants introduced into new countries where conditions seemed favourable for their growth have flourished so well that their luxuriance rivalled that of the plants growing in the land admitted to be their home. Support of the opposite view is sought in a Japanese legend which ascribes to China the honour of being the home of the tea plant; but, unfortunately, there is evidence for supposing that the Chinese never heard of this legend except from foreign sources, although the events related occurred in their own country. There are, however, certain references to the plant in the writings of a Celestial author who lived about 2,700 B.C. and a Chinese commentator of this ancient author, writing in the fourth century B.C., calls attention to the mention of the plant and adds that a beverage could be obtained from the leaves by adding hot water. It appears that the plant was used entirely as a medicine until A.D. 550, when it became a popular beverage.

EXERCISE 33

While we rest peacefully in our beds at night great machines are at work turning out thousands and sometimes millions of copies of our morning papers at the rate of four hundred or more copies a minute. Motors, trains and aeroplanes are carrying and distributing these newspapers to every part of the land ready for the house-to house delivery in the morning. The late hours of the night and the early hours of the morning are times of hard work for most of those who have any connexion with the first general distribution of newspapers. But so regularly does the paper appear at our door that we usually take it in and read it as a matter of course giving little or no thought to the means used to bring it to us or to the great care and planning and organisation behind its production. Success in the newspaper world depends in very large measure upon being on time. News which is late is generally news which has lost its value. Papers which are late are generally papers which will not be bought. All good newspaper men will tell us that in their trade there is little truth in the old saying "Better late than never."

All day long news and general information reaches the newspaper office. It is sent into the office by road and by railway, by sea and by air, by wire and by hand. Thousands of advertisements and hundreds of letters from readers are received daily and in addition there are pictures which are sent in the hope that they will appear next day on the picture page of the paper.

EXERCISE 34

Mass production is the name given to a
method of manufacture in which one standard pattern
takes the place of a variety of shapes and sizes. The
principle is not new, and its advantages have been
known in industry for a very long time. During the
last few decades, however, a number of manufacturers
have carried the method to its logical conclusion,
which is: one kind of article only produced in a
single factory. The advantages claimed for
the mass production method are many. Chief
among them is the possibility of adjusting the
operations of manufacture so that there may be the
completest economy in man and machine power

in every part of the work. The best known
example of mass production is the motor car, an
article which is complex and made of many parts.
The principle adopted is that of a series of factories
side by side in each of which a different part is
made. Those parts pass on in continuous streams
and on completion pass in to an assembly shop.
~~Here~~ the cars are gradually built up from the
beginning to the end at an almost incredible rate
of speed. From end to end the great saving
of thought, time, and labour arises from the
absolute similarity of one car to all others of the
same class. Every worker repeats ad infinitum the
operation that falls to him, till not a movement is
wasted or a fraction of time is lost

EXERCISE 35

To write is not necessarily to communicate
with another mind. Writing is primarily expression—
and whoever has made private use of it to record
what he has felt and thought and done, or to test
and amplify what he has heard or read, or as a
means of meditation, will know already that such
exercises are in themselves amply rewarding. He
will know also that, even if only as a preparation
for public communications, the practise of writing
to oneself is invaluable.

What are the main advantages of written expression?
As against thinking in the head, which is more likely
than not to be fragmentary and vague, the written
word gives a temporarily fixed form to the under-
lying thought it expresses, and so enables the
writer to judge whether the thought itself is of value
and whether its expression is adequate; while, as

against speech, the written word has possibilities of accuracy, subtlety, comprehensiveness and depth which would find it almost impossible to compass. A further advantage is that writing demands much more from us than the usual evanescent attention which limits our ordinary mental reactions to events. And, more than that, it compels us to bring together our still unrelated knowledge and makes us at the same time healthily, because acutely, aware of the gaps in it. Also by thus revealing us to ourselves, it offers us that self-knowledge without which there can be no effective self-direction. And, lastly, if we believe that developed minds are largely self-created, we realize at once that expression must be a main factor in their creation; for it is deeply true that if we never pass our experiences through the refining medium of written expression, not only do our feelings and thoughts and reasonings remain in a crude state, but mental development is retarded.

EXERCISE 36

Libel is a term which in popular use includes any
statement of a defamatory character made by one person of
another. Technically, however, it includes only statements
in writing or other more or less permanent record. Legally
spoken words are termed slander, and from the point of view
of the person complaining the distinction is important. In
the case of slander it is usually necessary to prove that
as a result of the words spoken the party claiming to be
injured has suffered special damage, whilst in libel such
proof is not necessary. Even in slander words imputing unfitness
dishonesty or incompetence in business or tending to prejudice
a man in his public calling are actionable without proof of
special damage. Even a public company may bring an

ation where defamation amounts to impeachment of its conduct of business.

Words spoken or written may on the face of them be innocent but they may have a hidden meaning understood by others. In such case the libel is by innuendo.

Fair comment on matters of public interest may be a justification of defamatory statements, and if the comment is fair and reasonable there is no libel. The standard of what is fair is not fixed but if the motive is pure the statement is generally justified, and the matter is a question of fact for the jury. Another justification is that the words spoken or written are true. This is a defence which must be proved to the hilt or the plea itself will aggravate the offence.

EXERCISE 37

Originally the work of professional
accountants was chiefly confined to the
checking of arithmetical accuracy of the
detailed records of transactoins in books
om account, the agreement of the trial
Balance, and the preparation of accounts;
in fact, to what may be described as
accountancy work, but nowadays the all
important part of a professional accountants work is that of auditing. The
difference between accountancy and auditing
is not clearly under stood by many business
men, it being thought that if accounts are
prepared by a professional accountent he
necessarily guarantees their accuracy.
This, however is far from being the case.

If accountant is instructed merely
to prepare accounts from a sets of books,
the work involved would be of agreeing

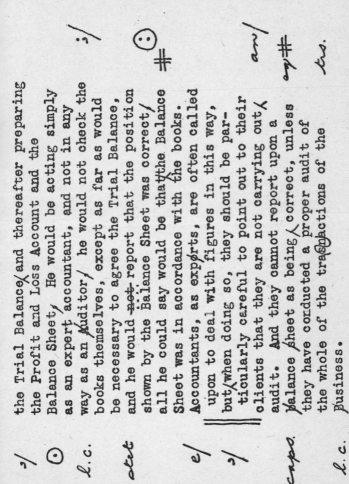

the Trial Balance and thereafter preparing
the Profit and Loss Account and the
Balance Sheet, He would be acting simply
as an expert accountant, and not in any
way as an Auditor, he would not check the
books themselves, except as far as would
be necessary to agree the Trial Balance,
and he would ~~not~~ report that the position
shown by the Balance Sheet was correct,
all he could say would be thatthe Balance
Sheet was in accordance with the books.
Accountants, as exports, are often called
upon to deal with figures in this way,
but when doing so, they should be particularly careful to point out to their
clients that they are not carrying out
audit. And they cannot report upon a
balance sheet as being correct, unless
they have conducted a proper audit of
the whole of the trasnactions of the
Business.

Signs Used for the Correction of Printers' Proofs.

	Apostrophe		Move to left
caps ≡	Capital letters		Move to right
→ centre	Centre	N.P.	New paragraph
	Close up	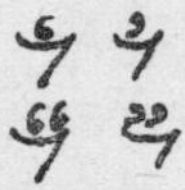	Quotation marks (single and double)
	Colon		Reverse or turn over
	Comma		Run on
	Delete		Semicolon
	Full stop		Space or more space to be left
	Hyphen	eq #	Spacing to be equalised
ital.	Italic type	stet.	"Let it stand"—do not omit parts struck out and dotted underneath
l.c.	Lower case—small letters	.....	"stet" (see above)
	Margin to be straightened	trs.	Transpose matter as marked
	Matter in margin to be inserted		Underscore—italics

SECTION XII

PUNCTUATION

CORRECT punctuation is an essential for the production of good typewritten work, and should be made the subject of special study. The styles followed by writers of reputation should be carefully observed and a textbook dealing with the subject obtained.

The examples given below show some of the chief uses of the various marks of expression which are arranged in alphabctical order. The portions in typewriter type should be copied several times.

Apostrophe (')

Three main functions of the apostrophe are the sign of the possessive case; an indication of contraction or omission; and the formation of plurals of letters and figures.

The possessive singular is indicated by adding 's.

```
The typist's chair.
Mr. Ward's typewriter.
Mr. Spring's desk.
Anderson's car.
```

By adding the apostrophe only, the possessive plural is indicated.

```
    Only seven days' notice is
required.
Six months' leave was granted.
```

When the plural form does not end in s, 's is added to form the possessive, as in *men's clothes*, *children's holidays*.

Possessive pronouns do not require the use of the apostrophe.

```
    Ours        Yours     Its
    Hers        This is ours
```

The omission of a letter is denoted by the insertion of the apostrophe.

```
    Don't     e'er     won't
```

In the case of plural formation of letters and figures the 's is added.

```
      Dot your i's and cross your
  t's.
  You don't sound your t's.
  Two 2's.
```

On the typewriter keyboard the apostrophe is usually represented by the single quotation mark.

Capitals

Names of persons, months, days, places, and book-titles are written with an initial capital letter.

```
John Brown, Esq.               England
New York        January        Tuesday
"Business Man's Guide"
```

Adjectives derived from proper names should be similarly treated.

```
    Indian         French Revolution
```

Some of these adjectives have, however, passed into common use, and no longer need a capital letter.

The initial letters of degrees and titles are usually typed with the capital letter.

B. A.	B. Com.	D. Sc.
LL. D.	Kt.	Bt.

Colon (:)

The colon, although separating parts of a compound sentence, indicates continuity of thought.

Be careful how you act: actions speak louder than words.

A longer pause is denoted by the colon than by the semicolon.

Important uses of the colon are to introduce quotations, lists, summaries, and explanations.

The following books are recommended: "Teach Yourself Mathematics," "Manual of Punctuation," "The Dictionary of Typewriting."

The lists may be run on or be typed in column form.

Colon and Dash (:—)

These are often used before a quotation or list that begins on a fresh line.

Comma (,)

The comma denotes the shortest pause or break in continuity.

> They live in houses, not in huts.

A short sentence of simple construction does not require commas.

> I shall go there tomorrow.

Between two long phrases joined by "and," the comma is usually inserted.

> We thank you for your letter, and have pleasure in accepting the offer.

Dash (—)

The dash may be used to indicate a break in a sentence. It is also used to separate items, as the contents of chapters of a book, and precedes definitions, explanations and illustrations.

> There are two kinds of spacing in typewriting - letter spacing and line spacing.

When typing the dash leave a space before and after.

Emphasis

The underscore can be used to emphasise a particular expression.

> We shall require copies <u>not later than Wednesday next</u>.

Exclamation, Note of (!)

An exclamation mark denotes an expression of wish or emotion.

```
Good luck!    Delightful!
```

Full Stop or Period (.)

This mark is used to note the end of a complete sentence which is neither a question nor an exclamation.

```
        Please reply to our previous
letter.
```

After most abbreviations and contractions the full stop is inserted.

```
Mr.   Messrs.   Staffs.   A.D.
```

The full stop is used as a decimal point, and to separate hours from minutes.

```
125.65      9.20 p.m.
```

Leader lines are made with the full stop. They may be typed continuously or in groups of two or three throughout the line.

```
20 copies .................. 15p
30 copies ..   ..   ..   ..  10p
40 copies ...  ...  ...  ...  8p
```

Hyphen (-)

This may show the relationship of two words forming a compound word.

```
Half-length      Self-contained
```

The hyphen is also used to mark division of a word

at the end of the line of writing, the remainder being carried to the beginning of the next line.

Nowadays the tendency is to use the hyphen as seldom as possible, and many words formerly hyphenated are now written as one word.

Interrogation, Note of (?)

This is used after a direct question.

```
        What is the price of the
Portable?
```

A question mark is not necessary when an order is given in the form of a question.

```
        Will you kindly let us have
the information as soon as pos-
sible.
```

Parenthesis ()

This is used to enclose subsidiary words, clauses, or sentences, to explain the leading idea of the sentence.

```
        The order to which you refer
(No. 16) has now been completed.
        Tinted typewriting papers
(usually of cheaper qualities)
are used chiefly for carbon
copies.
```

Square brackets—[]—are used to make further enclosure within a parenthesis, and also in legal work.

Parentheses should be used sparingly, to avoid awkward sentences.

Quotation Marks (“ ”)

The double quotation marks are used to enclose words exactly as quoted.

The inclusion of explanatory matter, as " he said," renders necessary the use of the quotation marks before and after the break.

> "I desire," he said, "to express my gratitude."

The quotation mark should not be placed at the beginning of every line of a quoted paragraph, only before the first word of each paragraph and at the end of the complete quotation.

Single quotation marks are used when a citation occurs within a citation, as the repetition of the double quotation marks would cause confusion.

Semicolon (;)

The use of the semicolon indicates a pause in a sentence where the second clause is too closely linked to the first to justify complete separation.

> There has been more than one postponement; and frequent consultations have taken place.

This mark is used between clauses of compound sentences.

> The girls attended the lectures; but the boys were not interested.

Exercises

In Exercises 38 and 39 several passages are given without punctuation marks and capital letters. Insert lightly in pencil the correct markings, and then type each section.

EXERCISE 38

in statistics it is sometimes convenient to express numerical fact pictorially and when this is done by means of a line drawn to scale we have a statistical graph the use of a graph is to present a comprehensive view of the numerical facts of a business or part of a business over a certain period

---

the strength of an organisation is the strength of its weakest joint one indifferent member of a team can cause considerable havoc in the work of the whole the management should see that each member of the staff pulls his weight and that each section functions in harmony with the rest much friction and inefficiency result from different departments under different heads each seeking and working for its own advantage

---

in the course of legal proceedings either of the parties may desire to make an effort to come to terms correspondence or interviews then take place and if it is made clear that the interviews are confidential or if the letters are marked without prejudice no use can be made of either as evidence if the case ever goes into court that is a letter written without prejudice can never be read except by leave of the party who has written it the reply to a letter thus marked is equally privileged

EXERCISE 39

nothing is so galling to a people not broken in from the birth as a paternal or in other words a meddling government a government which tells them what to read and say and eat and drink and wear our fathers could not bear it two hundred years ago and we are not more patient than they—*macaulay*

---

what i must do is all that concerns me not what the people think this rule equally arduous in actual and intellectual life may serve for thc whole distinction between greatness and meanness it is the harder because you will always find those who think they know what is your duty better than you know it—*emerson*

---

i have indeed lived nominally fifty years but deduct out of them the hours which i have lived to other people and not to myself and you will find me still a young fellow for that is the only true time which a man can properly call his own that which he has all to himself the rest though in some sense he may be said to live it is other peoples time not his the remnant of my poor days long or short is at least multiplied for me threefold my ten next years if i stretch so far will be as long as any preceding thirty—*lamb*

SECTION XIII

ENVELOPE ADDRESSING

THERE is no hard-and-fast rule for the addressing of envelopes; it is mainly a matter of individual preference. An important point, however, is observance of the Post Office suggestion that addresses should be legibly written in the lower part of the front of the envelope, with a clear margin above (not less than 1½ inches deep) for the postage stamps and postmarks. It is also of assistance to the postal authorities if capital letters are used for the name of the post town.

The envelopes should be placed on the left-hand side of the machine, so that each may be readily lifted with the left hand to be placed in position and fed in with the right hand by means of the cylinder knob.

There are two methods of addressing: "block" (each line beginning at the same point, as on p. 122) and "indented" (each line after the first beginning five spaces to the right of the preceding line, as on p. 121). The block method is most generally used, although for short line addresses the indented form is sometimes preferred.

On the ordinary business envelope the name of the addressee (the person or firm to whom the letter is being sent) should begin from one-third to half-way down the envelope, according to the length of the address, care being taken to finish the address at least half an inch from the bottom edge. Incorrectly addressed letters are often delayed in the post, and every care should be taken in the typing of addresses. Except in the case of very large towns, the name of the county should be included, and should be typed on a separate line.

The forms of address which occasion most difficulty are those for corporations, public bodies, and limited companies.

When there is an instruction for direction on the letter-heading, this should be carefully followed; it is not usual to address a Corporation official by name. A communication on general business would ordinarily be addressed to *The Town Clerk*, but departmental addresses may include *The Borough Treasurer*, *The Borough Engineer*, etc., or, in the case of a County Council, *The Clerk to the Council*. For a Government Department the address may begin *The Secretary*, *The Principal*, *The Controller*, etc.

For partnerships and limited companies the use of *Messrs.* requires special attention. *Messrs.* should be used when addressing a partnership, except when the name of the firm is preceded by the word *The*, or a title is included (examples—*Messrs. Brown & Jones*, *Messrs. Avis & Co.*, *The Regent Manufacturing Co.*, *Sir James Smith & Co.*). Hitherto, it has been the practice to use the courtesy title *Messrs.* before the title of a limited company when it contained personal names, and many people still prefer that form of address. A limited company, however, is an incorporated body—a legal person, distinct from any of its members—so that *Messrs.* is strictly out of place when used before the name of a limited company, and it is generally considered that communications should be addressed to an official of the company, such as *The Secretary*, *The General Manager*, etc.

Initials representing Christian names should be followed by a full stop and a space, but degrees and complimentary initials after a name, such as *M.A.*, *B.Sc.*, *M.B.E.*, are not divided by a space.

Supplementary notes placed on the envelope, such as *Personal*, *Urgent*, etc., should be typed at the bottom left-hand corner of the envelope, or immediately above the name of the addressee.

When " Junior " and " Senior " are required (father and son with same Christian name and at the same address), the abbreviations (*Jun.* or *Sen.*) are placed immediately after the name, as *Mr. Arthur Carey, Jun.*, or *Arthur Carey, Jun., Esq.*

Specimen forms of " block " and " indented " addresses are given on pp. 121 and 122, and in Exercises 40 and 41 lists of names and addresses (all fictitious) are provided for practice purposes. A folded sheet of paper, or any scrap of paper with an area of that of the ordinary envelope, will be suitable for practice. The reverse side of the front of any used envelope also provides excellent working paper.

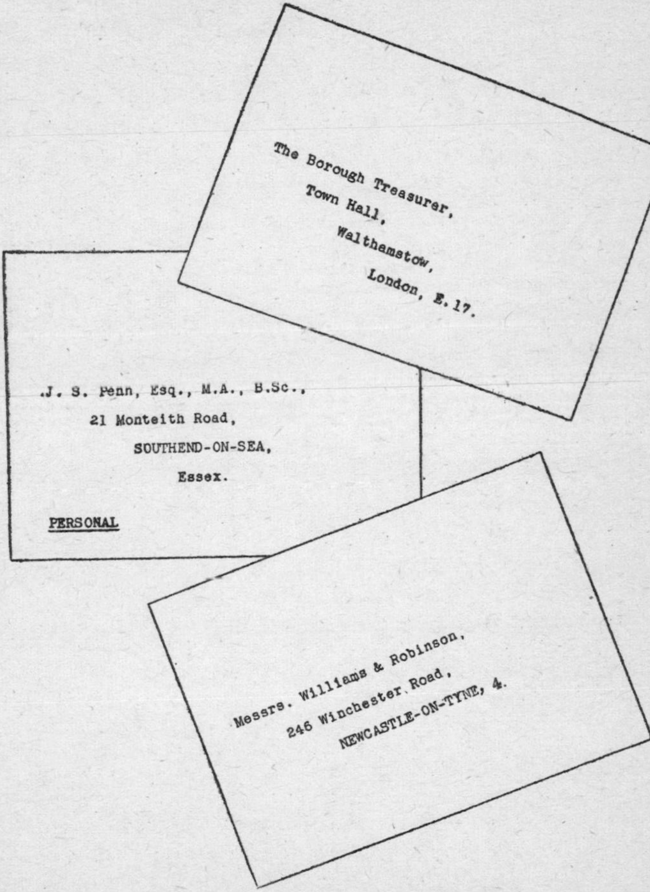

The Borough Treasurer,
Town Hall,
Walthamstow,
London, E.17.
J. S. Penn, Esq., M.A., B.Sc.,
21 Monteith Road,
SOUTHEND-ON-SEA,
Essex.
PERSONAL
Messrs. Williams & Robinson,
246 Winchester Road,
NEWCASTLE-ON-TYNE, 4.

Examples of "indented" form of address.

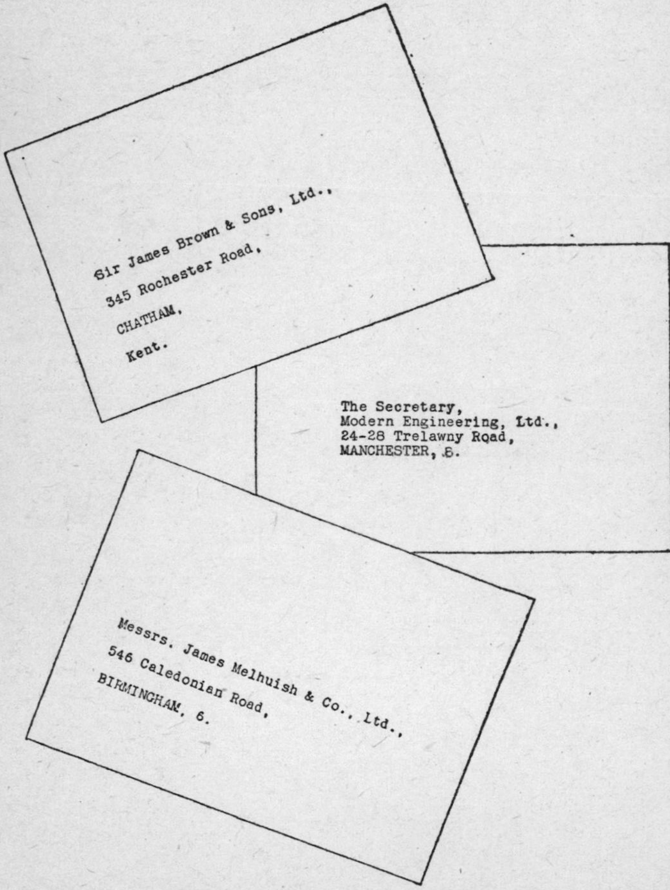

Sir James Brown & Sons, Ltd.,
345 Rochester Road,
CHATHAM,
Kent.
The Secretary,
Modern Engineering, Ltd.,
24-28 Trelawny Road,
MANCHESTER, 8.
Messrs. James Melhuish & Co., Ltd.,
546 Caledonian Road,
BIRMINGHAM, 6.

Examples of "block" form of address.

EXERCISE 40

(Type the following addresses in " block " form, with any additions necessary.)

William Mason & Co., Ltd., Aston Road, Sheffield, 6.

The Secretary, The Acme Engineering Co., Ltd., College Road, Birmingham, 7.

John Laughton, M.D., 36 Dudley Road, Derby.

S. W. Kemp & Sons, 26–30 Booth Street, Northampton.

Robert Macdonald, 145 Ladywood Road, Portsmouth.

Major Herbert Wilson, D.S.O., Bridge Avenue, Reading, Berks.

Professor Sir Albert Lawrence, Melville Lodge, Coventry.

J. N. C. Allerton, 29 Whitmore Road, Plymouth.

E. Griffiths & Co., Ltd., Exeter Street, Newmarket.

Arthur W. Odell, 63 Charlton Hill, Chester.

Sir Arthur Freeman & Sons, Ltd., Compton Road, Bournemouth, Hants.

Robert Grant, Jun., Belmont Road, Falmouth.

Sir William Meston, Bt., Victoria Square, Bath.

R. C. Marshall & Sons, Ltd., 36–40 Lawrence Road, London, E.17.

The Rt. Hon. Sir J. Hammond, 84 Havelock Terrace, Edinburgh.

H. Melhuish & Co., Ltd., Preston Street, Huddersfield, Yorks.

Herbert Barnard, Sen., 41 Princes Road, Eastbourne, Sussex.

EXERCISE 41

(*Type the following addresses in " indented " form, with any additions necessary.*)

F. T. Pemberton & Co., Ltd., 42–48 Ashley Road, Dover, Kent.

The Bridge Manufacturing Co., Ltd., Claremont Road, Gloucester.

Mrs. Elsie Davidson, 29 Stapleton Road, Greenwich, London, S.E.10.

John W. Whitney, 124 Wellington Avenue, Stratford on Avon.

The Manager, Harvey & Sims, Ltd., West Street, Belfast.

T. & F. Stanford, Ltd., Brunswick Works, Willesden, London, N.W.10.

The Rev. William Gardner, M.A., The Rectory, Grange Road, Norwich.

Sir William Young & Sons, Ltd., Stanhope Place, Lincoln.

J. Wyatt & Sons, Ltd., Manor Road, Victoria Street, London, S.W.1.

The Midland Optical Co., Ltd., Western Road, Birmingham.

James W. Fielding, B.Com., 94 Newton Road, Newcastle-on-Tyne.

The Managing Director, Gerald Dennis & Sons, Ltd., Mayfield Road, West Bromwich, Staffs.

Dobson & Brown, 34 Burnham Terrace, Liverpool, 1.

J. W. Penn, M.A., Chapel Road, Brighton, Sussex.

Major-General Sir Alfred Gilbert, Cathcart Crescent, Glasgow, C.2.

SECTION XIV

CORRESPONDENCE—CARBON COPYING

ONE of the most important duties of typists is the preparation of correspondence for signature, as the greatest part of the world's business is conducted through the post. These letters convey their messages more effectively if they are attractively produced.

The chief characteristics of a good letter are clearness, accuracy, brevity, and courtesy. There are various components of a business letter, and in the paragraphs which follow each portion is dealt with.

Sizes of Letter Paper

The standard sizes are *quarto* (8″ × 10″) and *foolscap* (8″ × 13″). For very short letters and private correspondence *octavo* (8″ × 5″) is used. The new International Paper Sizes of A4 and A5 are now taking over (see p. 24).

Letter Headings

These headings are generally the product of the printer, and are tastefully prepared to be in keeping with the class of business. The details given in the letter heading include, in bold display type, the name and business of the firm, the address from which that business is conducted, telephone numbers, telegraphic address, etc. For private correspondence the letter paper usually contains the address, telephone number, and the name of the nearest railway station (or omnibus route). Specimen letter headings are reproduced with the examples on pp. 134–137. The names are, of course, fictitious.

Width of Margins

Margin widths are governed largely by individual preference and the length of the letter, and the margin stops should be set before commencing work. At one time the widths of the margin usually allowed were $1\frac{1}{2}''$ on the left and $1''$ on the right, the wider left-hand margin being a survival from the days when this was considered as the filing margin. Nowadays, however, with an open filing system, the practice is to allow even margins, to secure a centred effect on the paper, in much the same way as the printed page of a book.

Insertion of Date

The order recommended is day, month, and year typed on one line, as:

```
17th April, 19--
```

An examination of business correspondence will on occasion show two and three line variations of presentation, and, although they are often well displayed, the method is not time-saving.

Insert the date immediately below the printed address, so as not to extend beyond the right-hand margin of the body of the letter. Another method is to centre the date, but a great deal will depend upon the layout of the letter heading.

A date line was at one time inserted, but it is now seldom seen. Its deletion is recommended, as the necessary adjustment with the variable line spacer results in a loss of time, and the typewritten matter is often out of alignment.

Reference Initials

In business correspondence these references usually consist of the initials of the dictator and the typist, as DF/OH. Alternatively a departmental number may be used, as SALES /916. If a place has not been allotted for these details in the printed letter heading, they can be placed at the left-hand margin, and on the same line as the date. This gives a balanced effect. Sometimes the initials are inserted at the end of the letter. When replying to a correspondent do not forget to include his reference. It will be helpful to him in dealing with the letter—that is the reason for its insertion.

Addressee

The addressee is the person or firm to whom the letter is being sent, and the name and address are in most cases placed at the beginning of the letter. The first line of these details should begin at the point decided upon for the left-hand margin, and subsequent lines may be indented (begin five spaces to the right of the preceding line), or the whole address may be in block form (each line level with the margin). Single-line spacing should be used, and, when possible, the name and address should be limited to three lines; it is not necessary for each item to occupy a separate line. Every care should be taken to ensure that the name of the correspondent is given correctly. Many people are sensitive about the misspelling of their names, although their illegible handwriting may be a contributory cause of the error.

Salutation

The opening to a letter is termed the " salutation," and the forms used include:

Dear Sir,	Madam,	Sirs,
Dear Sirs,	Dear Madam,	Gentlemen,

Type the salutation two or three line spaces below the inside address, and follow with a comma. In private correspondence the salutation and the complimentary close are often handwritten, to give a more personal effect.

Subject Heading

When a subject heading is required, place it immediately above the body of the letter and in the middle of the writing line. The heading should be underlined by means of the underscore, and, when there are two or more in a letter, they should be centred over each section or placed at the beginning of the left-hand margin (see examples on pp. 134 and 136 and Centring, p. 154). Unless the heading ends with an abbreviation, a full stop should not be inserted after it.

Body of Letter

This contains the subject-matter of the letter, and it is the general practice to indent the first line of each paragraph five spaces. Single-line spacing should be used, with double-line spacing for very short letters. There should in either case be double-line spacing between the paragraphs, and the tabulator stop should be set for the paragraph indentation.

Endeavour to cultivate the art of paragraphing. A solid letter of one paragraph makes difficult reading. Where several distinct subjects are dealt with in a letter, division into paragraphs will occasion little difficulty, and by examining the paragraphing of newspaper articles and correspondence this art can be quickly and efficiently developed.

Do not use the ampersand (&) for "and" in the

body of the letter, unless reference is made to the name of a firm, or numbers are being quoted.

Continuation Sheets

These may be necessary when a letter occupies more than one sheet of paper, and they should be of the same size and quality as the letter heading. Continuation sheets are not usually printed with the firm's letter heading. The details required across one line, *evenly displayed* at the top of the second sheet, are the name of the addressee, the number of the page, and the date as:

R. Kelly, Esq. (2) 17th April, 19--

Do not use a continuation sheet for only two lines. A readjustment of margins may make it possible to type the letter on one sheet.

Complimentary Close

This termination (sometimes called " the subscription ") is typed two line spaces below the final paragraph of the letter, and should begin at the middle of the line of writing. Those most used are:

Yours faithfully,	Yours truly,
Faithfully yours,	Yours very truly,
Yours sincerely,	Yours obediently,

Name of the Firm or Company

Capital letters are used for the name of the company following the complimentary close, and the letter may be signed by a member of the staff who acts as an agent.

The name of the company may be prefaced by the word " for." The abbreviated form of *per procurationem*—*per pro.* or *p.p.*—is also used.

The Signature

This will be handwritten, and, when the official position of the writer is placed after the complimentary close, sufficient space should be left for the insertion of the signature. The designation (" Secretary," " Manager," etc.) should end within the right-hand margin.

Enclosures

The indication of enclosures to a letter is given by typing the abbreviated form `Enc.` or `2 Encs.` in the space which may be provided for this information, or at the bottom left-hand corner of the letter. (If there is room `Enc.` should be typed two or three line spaces below the designation.) Labels are sometimes affixed to the letter and a duplicate placed on the enclosure. In official and legal correspondence a mark may be made in the margin on the same line as the reference to an enclosure.

Layout Diagram

On p. 133 the layout for a letter is given in diagrammatic form, together with a key to the sections. The dotted outline represents the letter heading. A layout in that form will give a well-balanced letter. A word of warning, however, is necessary. If there are any special " rules of the house " regarding the display of letters, the wishes of the principal should be observed.

Exercises

The exercises which follow give examples of many business letters. Each letter should be typed accurately, and fictitious references and the date should be inserted.

CARBON COPYING

For business transactions it is desirable to have a record of documents despatched, and there are various methods of copying letters, etc. That most popular is the carbon-paper method; the copies are made at the same time as the original. The number of copies that can be secured by this means will depend upon the typewriter used and on the quality of the typewriting paper.

Normally carbon paper can be obtained in a variety of sizes and colours, and single-sided carbons (coated on one side) are mostly used.

In preparing to take carbon copies, the first sheet should be placed face downward on the table. On this a sheet of carbon paper should be placed with the coated surface upward; then another sheet of paper, another carbon, and so on for the required number. See that the carbon sheets are in correct position, so that all of the original appears on the copies.

When the sheets are inserted in the machine, care should be taken to see that the coated side of the sheet faces the cylinder, and the pressure of the feed-rolls should be released by depressing the paper release lever, particularly when there are several sheets. The pressure can be restored when the top edges of the sheets have passed the feed-rolls. This pressure should also be released when the sheets are withdrawn from the machine.

Corrections on Carbon Copies

One method of correction is to place a small piece of paper between each carbon and its copy at the point where the erasure is made. First make the erasure on the top copy; then lift the first carbon and remove the small piece of paper and erase the error from the carbon copy; then lift the second carbon and follow the same procedure until all the sheets have been dealt with. Before typing the correction all the pieces of paper must be removed.

Another method of correction is to mark the errors in pencil and to erase each error when the paper has been removed from the machine on completion of the work. Each sheet will then have to be re-inserted separately for the corrections to be made, and to secure the carbon appearance on the copies, place a piece of carbon paper at the printing point when typing the corrections.

Carbon Economy

Wastage of carbon sheets can be avoided by reversing them immediately there is sign of wear, the bottom being placed at the top for subsequent copies. When one particular area has been in fairly constant use, the remainder may be practically untouched. Alternatively, cut away a small portion of the top edge, so that when the trimmed edge is placed at the top of the paper an additional unused surface becomes available.

PRINTED HEADING

(1) ....

(2) ....
....
....

(3) ....

(4) ....

(5) ....
....
....

(5) ....
....
....

(6) ....
(7) ....

(8) ....

(9) ....

(10) ....

The numbers refer to the following sections of the letter: (1) Date; (2) Name and address of addressee; (3) Salutation; (4) Subject Heading; (5) Paragraphs in body of letter; (6) Complimentary close; (7) Firm name; (8) Signatory's designation; (9) Reference; (10) Enclosure.

10 May 19..

Messrs John Cross & Co
235-239 High Street
Sheffield 1

Dear Sirs

<u>ROLLER BOOK BACKING MACHINE</u>

We are contemplating the installation of one of these machines, 13 ins wide, and shall be glad to know what is your lowest price and when you can deliver a machine.

For some years we have had one of your machines of this size in constant use here, and it has always given us great satisfaction.

We shall be glad to have a reply at your earliest convenience.

Yours faithfully
MOORLANDS & JOHNSON LTD

Director

Ref: EMD/AE

Example of an <u>indented</u> style, with subject heading.

24 March 19..

Messrs Plummer & Co
841 Market Street
St Albans, Herts

Dear Sirs

We shall be grateful if you will send us a quotation for producing 50,000 copies of our price list, in accordance with the attached specification.

We enclose a copy of the one previously issued, which was produced for us by another firm of printers, and we shall be glad if you will follow this for general style.

We wish to have this price list ready for distribution at the earliest possible moment, and shall appreciate anything you can do to help us.

Yours faithfully
for WHITEHEAD & SAUNDERS LTD

Manager

Ref: AD/DW

Enc

12 December 19..

Stanley Kelly Esq
345 Charter Road
Ilford
Essex

Dear Sir

YOURSELF v GOODMAN

The defendant has entered an appearance to the writ served upon him, and his solicitor called upon us this afternoon. He informs us that his client disputes the last three items of your claim, and is prepared to defend the action unless a compromise can be arrived at. He offered without prejudice to pay £200, if you will accept that sum in settlement of debt and costs, by four monthly instalments of £50 each.

We shall be glad to hear from you whether or not you are disposed to agree to these terms. If you are not it would be as well to proceed without delay, and in that case it will be necessary for you to make an affidavit in proof of the debt, so that we may at once take out a summons for leave to sign judgment, notwithstanding the appearance.

On the hearing of the application the defendant will, if he intends to persist in his contention with reference to the last three items of the account, have to satisfy the Master by affidavit that he has reasonable grounds of defence, and the probability is that he will be granted leave to defend only on condition of his bringing into court the amount admitted to be owing.

If you would like to discuss the matter with us before deciding, we should be pleased to see you here tomorrow morning.

Yours faithfully

DW/RT

Ref: ATN/MG 10 May, 19..

Messrs. H. Blakemore & Sons,
167 Wordsworth Road,
Reading, Berks.

Dear Sirs,

We have your letter of yesterday's date, and are prepared to grant you an agency for the sale of our goods on the following terms:

(1) We will allow you a commission of 20 per cent off catalogue prices on all goods purchased by you or through your agency, and also a discount of 5 per cent on accounts paid within one month from date of invoice. You are, however, to forgo discount on accounts not paid within three months.

(2) We will undertake not to grant another agency in your district.

(3) We will furnish you with catalogues periodically, setting out particulars and prices, and bearing your name and address as district agents, together with leaflets with your name and address printed thereon.

(4) We will send goods to your premises packed and carriage paid.

If the above terms are satisfactory to you, we shall be pleased to discuss the matter further.

Yours faithfully,
for J. ANDREW & CO., LTD.

Example of semi-blocked letter, with indentations in body of letter.

EXERCISE 42

The Borough Treasurer,
Town Hall,
Lendham, Bucks.

Dear Sir,

I have available certain trust moneys for investment in Corporation security, and shall be obliged if you will state your terms for an investment not exceeding £15,000.

My clients, who are anxious to place a loan at an early date, have not yet finally decided upon the duration of the investment, and therefore I shall be pleased to receive offers for a long-term and a short-term loan.

Yours faithfully,

EXERCISE 43

The Secretary,
The Bridge Machinery Co.,
Garner Road,
Stockport, Cheshire.

Dear Sir,

It is unfortunate, as you acknowledge, that we are having a great deal of trouble with the "Crosford" machine which you installed last month. We assure you that our maintenance engineer has acted in accordance with your suggestions, but without securing satisfactory results.

In the circumstances, we shall be pleased if you will arrange to send your expert on Thursday morning, if possible, to inspect the machine and to advise us.

Yours faithfully,

EXERCISE 44

Messrs. Andrews & Son,
14–16 Church Street,
Liverpool, 3.

Dear Sirs,

Your inquiry, for which we thank you, interests us. We are sorry that we are unable to let you have a quotation by return as there is insufficient time for us to look up essential details. We will, however, write to you fully on Friday next without fail.

In the meantime, we shall be pleased if you will give us additional particulars by filling in the attached form and returning it at once to this office.

Yours faithfully,

Enc.

EXERCISE 45

The General Manager,
Brick & Steel, Ltd.,
Palace Wharf,
Edgware, Middx.

Dear Sir,

You are invited to tender for the erection of a block of flats at Main Avenue, London, W.1, for The Housing Trust, Ltd., and I shall be pleased if you will let me know as soon as possible whether you desire to tender, in order that the quantities may be sent to you. The drawings of the proposed work may be inspected at my office on making an appointment.

Tenders are to be delivered to me within one month.

Yours faithfully,

EXERCISE 46

The General Manager,
Machinery Components, Ltd.,
Corporation Road,
Littleshaw, Lancs.

Dear Sir,

At a meeting of the Board held today the question of disposing of two of our Quad Demy machines and replacing them with two new machines of similar size was under consideration.

I have been asked to inquire of you the best price you would allow for one of the old machines and also whether you would make a proportionately larger allowance in the event of my Board deciding upon the installation of two machines instead of one.

The serial numbers of the old machines are Z.865 and Z.898.

Yours faithfully,

Managing Director

EXERCISE 47

The Secretary,
Climax Steel Co., Ltd.,
Sheffield, 19.

Dear Sir,

We are sending herewith our Order No. 608 for Steel Angles and Channels, which we are urgently requiring in connexion with an important contract. Delivery is of extreme importance and we should like to have the material in our Works by next week-end if possible.

The bars to be supplied would be of ordinary commercial quality, and while the quantity is large you will observe that there are only three sections involved. In these circumstances we have no doubt you will be able to meet our requirements in regard to delivery.

Please let us know by return the very best you can do for us.

Yours faithfully,

Enc.

EXERCISE 48

Messrs. Benham & Brown,
417 Selwyn Road,
London, E.17.

Dear Sirs,

We confirm our conversation on the telephone to-day. The fittings referred to in your letter of yesterday were received, but, unfortunately, one of the crates appears to have been dropped during transit, as many of the contents were either broken or cracked. A list of the damaged articles is enclosed, and we shall be glad if you will kindly arrange to send replacements as soon as possible.

We are placed in a rather awkward position regarding the goods in BX/739 crate which was badly damaged. To complete a rush order we are in urgent need of two more, and we understand that you are making arrangements for these to be despatched to our Works with all possible speed.

Yours faithfully,

Enc.

EXERCISE 49

The Secretary,
The Boden Machinery Co.,
Waterloo Road,
Bristol, 7.

Dear Sir,

Messrs. Jones & Wilkins inform us that they purchased equipment from you a year ago, and it is at their suggestion that we are writing to you in connexion with our need for various types of machinery.

We shall be glad, therefore, if you will let us have your catalogue and details of the most modern equipment you have for food manufacturers. At the moment, we have our own generating station, and run two vertical boilers and one horizontal boiler.

It is intended to begin production as early as possible, and we can let you have details of our proposed weekly output as soon as we have had an opportunity of considering the various types of plant you have to offer.

Yours faithfully,

EXERCISE 50

The Secretary,
The Art Metal Co., Ltd.,
Hart Street,
Manchester, 16.

Dear Sir,

We enclose drawings of a proposed shop front and shall be pleased to have your keenest quotation for the material specified, fitted ready for assembly, including transport charges to Liverpool.

Full-sized detail is indicated for the bronze metal work, but we do not insist on strict adherence to this so long as you quote for sections of a simple nature. We would draw your attention to the metal bars over the doorway, which are to be ornamental but inexpensive. Two of these bars should be drilled to permit of numerals being fixed. Do not include in your quotation the cost of metal numerals and door handles.

We are anxious to get this contract under way, and shall be glad to have an early reply.

Yours faithfully,

Encs.

EXERCISE 51

Messrs. Pelham & Son,
Winchester Road,
Newcastle-on-Tyne, 14.

Dear Sirs,

We thank you for your inquiry of yesterday, and are ready to supply you with the cloth in question at 25p a yard.

A comparison of this figure with the market price will convince you that our quotation could not be bettered elsewhere. In anticipation of a large order we have cut our price to a point where the margin of profit is almost insignificant; with this fact in mind you will, of course, expect no discount for payment within seven days.

It is not our intention to rush you into a decision, but, as our stocks are low enough to be exhausted by two or three large orders, we would advise you in your own interests to give us telephonic instructions if you wish to avail yourselves of this offer.

Yours faithfully,

EXERCISE 52

Messrs. Kitchener & Co.,
Station Street,
Birmingham, 8.

Dear Sirs,

We have now considered the question of advertising discussed at our interview last week, and, before reaching a decision on the illustrations, we should be glad if you would submit one or two finished drawings as specimens of the type to be used throughout the campaign.

The copy for the advertisement is enclosed, but we should be glad if your copywriter could strengthen it considerably.

We realise that it would be too expensive a proposition to secure solus positions for the smaller advertisements that we shall be using later in the campaign, but we should be glad if you would instruct your space-buyer to use his influence to obtain these wherever possible, especially in the provinces.

Yours faithfully,

Enc.

EXERCISE 53

Messrs. Waterson Bros.,
Richmond Road,
Cardiff.

Dear Sirs,

We are urgently in need of two petrol engines suitable for driving a 6′ mortar-mill or a 12″ × 6″ stone-breaker. At present we have three engines in daily operation, but require two additional engines to cope with an important contract we have just concluded for work on the new by-pass road under construction here.

The work is scheduled for completion within the next eight months, and we feel we have no time to lose. We trust, therefore, that you can fill our requirements, and also give us early delivery.

The three engines mentioned as being already in use are of the well known Benson make, but, as the makers of our mortar-mill and stone-breaker have strongly recommended your own engines to several of our travellers, we should like to try them out.

Please let us have the necessary information at your early convenience.

Yours faithfully,

EXERCISE 54

William Mortimore, Esq.,
The Cedars,
Harrogate, Yorkshire.

Dear Sir,

We are very glad that you have written to us to query some of the items on the bill that we submitted to you, since we always urge customers to write to let us know when they do not feel satisfied upon any matter.

With regard to the oil which you state is very much dearer than before, we would mention that you agreed a better grade of oil would conserve the engine-power for a longer period, and you authorised us to supply you with a more expensive brand.

The service charge of one pound for repair to the front off mudguard was undertaken at the order of your son.

We regret that we are not able to reduce the charge for the materials, as this was previously agreed upon as being reasonable.

Yours faithfully,

EXERCISE 55

Messrs. John Smith & Co.,
901 London Road,
Maidstone, Kent.

Dear Sirs,

The steady growth of our business has rendered imperative an early move to more commodious premises. Our old factory has rapidly become unable to cope efficiently with the increased demands, and to ensure satisfactory service a large building at Main Street, Slough, Bucks, has been taken over.

The site is a particularly good one, in the heart of this industrial centre, within easy reach of the railway, the road, and the canal. Transport difficulties are thus reduced to a minimum, and early deliveries ensured.

The new factory offers great scope for mechanical improvements, and a resulting increase in both the quantity and the quality of our output is confidently expected.

Transitional periods are, as you will realise, attended with considerable difficulty; we trust that you will in the circumstances allow us a certain amount of indulgence. As the factory will be ready for production within a fortnight, we can assure you of the prompt delivery of all goods ordered a week hence.

We take this opportunity of expressing our thanks for your confidence in the past, and we hope that the improvements we shall introduce will lead to even more business.

Yours faithfully,

EXERCISE 56

The General Manager,
J. Finn & Co., Ltd.,
534 Western Road,
Swindon, Wiltshire.

Dear Sir,

We should be pleased to assist you to the best of our ability to replenish your stock on advantageous terms.

The enclosed illustrated catalogue contains concise details of many household goods that we think would interest you.

We have just been appointed agents for the manufacturers of a British-made Oil Heater which is both cheap and satisfactory, and your special inquiry reaches us at the right moment. The heater is obtainable in various models at prices from £4·50, and has the following special points:

(1) It gives a maximum heat of twice as much warmth as other heaters in its class.
(2) The flame is easily adjustable to any reasonable height, giving greatly increased comfort and economy.
(3) With the patent burner any excess of oil is drained back into the tank, ensuring safety and complete elimination of smoke and smell.
(4) The heater burns at full capacity for a cost of approximately 1p an hour.

If you will let us know your requirements we will instruct our representative to call upon you.

Yours faithfully,

Enc.

EXERCISE 57

Joseph Grant, Esq.,
Alma Road, Tottenham,
London, N.17.

Dear Sir,

We had the pleasure last week of submitting for your inspection samples of our latest designs in Tapestries and Curtain Materials. We understand from our representative's report that you were pleased with the patterns and quality and that you found our prices reasonable.

We are, therefore, disappointed to find that we have not yet received your order, as we feel certain that no better value can be obtained anywhere in the lines we offered you.

Our representative has suggested that you may require longer credit terms than we are in the habit of allowing. If this is so, we are prepared to consider any suggestion you may care to make.

We enclose patterns of two designs that arrived this week. The higher-priced pattern is our own exclusive design and will be supplied to one retailer only in each district; as a special inducement to you to open an account with us, we are giving you the first offer of this material.

Please do not hesitate to write or telephone if you have any inquiry to make.

Yours faithfully,

Enc.

EXERCISE 58

The General Manager,
James Penn & Sons, Ltd.,
290 Charter Road,
Rochester, Kent.

Dear Sir,

In reply to your letter of yesterday, we shall be glad to have the opportunity of quoting for the production of your catalogue. We have cast off the copy, and find that you have seriously under-estimated the number of pages.

In view of the fact that considerable handling is indicated, we consider the book should be cut flush, and we also suggest rounded instead of square corners, as less likely to curl up. Although white art paper is inclined to show wear rather quickly, and is more expensive than imitation art or super-calendered, we presume there will be a number of half-tone illustrations, and we therefore think it advisable to use white art. This will bring out the half-tones much more impressively, and provide a more pleasing and attractive appearance. If, however, you decide to use the cheaper papers, we recommend you to reduce the vignetting of the blocks to a minimum, as this will make it easier for us to get a good result.

In connexion with type faces, we are sending you our book of specimens, and suggest that you go through this and pick out the types you recommend.

Yours faithfully,

Enc.

EXERCISE 59

The General Manager,
Adkins & Co., Ltd.,
248 Roberts Road,
Huddersfield, Yorkshire.

Dear Sir,

We have now definitely decided to establish a

factory in Huddersfield, providing that a suitable site can be found, and that there is no shortage of the necessary skilled labour in the district.

We are prepared to entrust to you the task of prospecting for a satisfactory position, and to leave to your judgment any urgent decisions that may have to be taken.

Please let us know whether there is likely to be any difficulty over finding employees with the specialised experience that is demanded in our own particular line of business, and whether there is any danger of neighbouring firms competing with us in wage levels.

It is as yet too early to go fully into questions of staff, but executive officials will for the most part be sent from here, and in this connexion we have in mind, amongst others, our Assistant Sales Manager, Mr. J. Barlow, who joined us some time ago.

In launching an enterprise of this sort it is realised that it is essential to have the advice of others who possess an intimate knowledge of the market.

We hope that you will do your best to make the various arrangements as speedily as possible as we are anxious to have the factory at work within the next twelve months.

Yours faithfully,

SECTION XV

DISPLAY WORK

DISPLAY work involves the neat and orderly arrangement of the text so that the complete typewritten work will be pleasing to the eye and also easily read.

Printed Matter as Guide

The work of the printer can be taken as a guide, but, owing to the uniformity of type fitted to the typewriter, the typist can only in a small way approximate to the work of the printer, who has a wide selection of type-faces to choose from, and also has facilities for ornamenting his composition.

There are many different ways of securing emphasis and an attractive display of typewritten work, and it is here that the operator can exercise artistic taste. The ability to display effectively is to some extent a natural gift, although it can be acquired by a careful study of the work of others, both in typewriting and in print. Ideas obtained in this way can be improved upon or adapted to secure an attractive display.

Borders and Rules

Skill is needed in the use of initial capitals and capitals and small letters, spaced and unspaced, underscoring, variations of line spacing, and the distribution of white space. Too much emphasis, however, is worse than none at all, and this applies particularly to underscoring. Freak arrangements and the elaborate use of decorative effects are usually avoided in business, but borders and rules can be arranged attractively. The best effect is obtained with little or no ornamentation and extreme simplicity. The following are examples:

```
__________________________________
: : : : : : : : : : : : : : : : : : : : : : : : : : : : : : : : : :
__________________________________

__________________________________
----------------------------------
__________________________________

__________________________________
xxxxxxxxxxxxxxxxxxxxxxxxxxxxxxxxxx
__________________________________
```

Centring

Display work is to a large extent a question of accurate centring, the text being arranged in such a way that there is equal space on either side of the typewritten matter. It is not, however, desirable to centre everything, and this point can be appreciated by observing the methods adopted in display advertisements.

One method of centring is, first, to count the number of letters and spaces to be occupied by the heading, and then to subtract the total from the number of spaces in the line of writing or the width of the paper. For quarto paper, eight inches wide and using Pica type, the total is eighty. Take, as an example for centring, the title of this handbook—

TEACH YOURSELF TYPEWRITING

The number of spaces to be allowed is twenty-six, and deducted from eighty gives a remainder of fifty-four. This number divided by two shows the point of the scale (27) at which the line should begin. Should the division result in a fraction, the next highest number will be the starting point.

When the heading is to be placed over matter which has unequal margins, the matter will be arranged immediately over the width of the line of writing, not the width of the paper. If, for example, for binding purposes there is a left-hand margin of fifteen and a right-hand margin of five (or a writing line of sixty spaces), the above book title would begin at 32 on the scale.

Back Spacer for Centring

Another method of finding the middle of the line is to set the carriage position indicator at 40 (assuming that quarto paper has been inserted at zero), and then to back space once for every two letters or spaces in the heading. To centre the same book-title it would be necessary to depress the back spacer thirteen times. By many this repeated use of the back spacer is not recommended, as it is considered that this key is for slight adjustments only—one or two spaces.

Tail Pieces

A decorative effect is sometimes desired at the end of chapters or sections, and arrangements of characters suitable for this purpose are:

---ooOoo---   ---:::::---   --xxXxx--

Display Examples

The best examples of display work are to be found in printed matter, chiefly handbills, title-pages, notices, programmes, menus, etc., and the examples on pp. 157 to 160 are given as being representative of work that can be accomplished on the typewriter.

In Exercise 60 various items are given for centring

practice; count the number of letters and spaces required for each, and then type them successively in the middle of a quarto sheet of paper. Where there is a space between the letters in a word, it is customary to leave *three* spaces between the words.

EXERCISE 60

GREATER LONDON COUNCIL

CITY OF LONDON

BRITISH RAIL

HER MAJESTY'S STATIONERY OFFICE

LONDON TRANSPORT EXECUTIVE

BOARD OF TRADE JOURNAL

POST OFFICE GUIDE

RAILWAY EXECUTIVE

BALANCE SHEET

PROFIT AND LOSS ACCOUNT

LONDON CHAMBER OF COMMERCE

ROYAL SOCIETY OF ARTS

THE TIMES

DAILY EXPRESS

DAILY MAIL

THE DICTIONARY OF TYPEWRITING

////////////////////////////////////

THE R E I S A F I R E

E V E R Y O T H E R M I N U T E

You can't be too careful!

////////////////////////////////////

X-X-X-X-X-X-X-X-X-X-X-X-X-X-X-X-X-X

C O U G H S a n d S N E E Z E S

S P R E A D D I S E A S E S

Trap the germs in your handkerchief

X-X-X-X-X-X-X-X-X-X-X-X-X-X-X-X-X-X

ooo-ooo-ooo-ooo-ooo-ooo-ooo-ooo-ooo

(give the exact fare
P L E A S E (
(name your destination

H E L P T H E C O N D U C T O R

ooo-ooo-ooo-ooo-ooo-ooo-ooo-ooo-ooo

xxxxxxxxxxxxxxxxxxxxxxxxxxxxxxxxxxxxxxxxxxx

---- M U S I C ----

1.	Overture	Life's Laughter	Rust
2.	Selection	Mikado	Sullivan
3.	Waltz	Bal Masque	Fletcher
4.	Suite	Carmen	Bizet
5.	Selection	Rose Marie	Friml
6.	Intermezzo	Longing	Haydn Wood
7.	Waltz	Count of Luxembourg	Lehar
8.	Selection	Merrie England	German
9.	Suite	The Royal Fireworks	Handel
10.	Entr'acte	Lovely Night	Ganne
11.	Waltz	The Song is Ended	Berlin
12.	Selection	Scotch Airs	Myddleton

THE "ELITE" ORCHESTRA
under the direction of
MISS EILEEN NIGHTINGALE

xxxxxxxxxxxxxxxxxxxxxxxxxxxxxxxxxxxxxxxxxxx

K N I G H T S O F T H E

R O U N D T A B L E

FIVE PLAYS FROM THE
ARTHURIAN LEGEND

by

L. du GARDE PEACH

---oOo---

LONDON

Sir Isaac Pitman & Sons, Ltd.

M E N U

Soup

Consommé Royale
Thick Oxtail

Fish

Fillets Lemon Sole
Tartare Sauce

Joints

Braised Sweetbreads and Macédoine
Roast Chicken and Sausage

Vegetables

Spinach New Potatoes

Sweets

Trifle Peach Melba

Coffee

SECTION XVI

TABULAR WORK

THE work in this section is really an extension of the previous instructions regarding the display and the centring of typewritten matter, and deals mainly with the orderly arrangement of headings over wide or narrow columns of words or figures.

Tabular work is undoubtedly one of the most difficult branches of typewriting, and requires very careful planning to secure the most effective results. The endeavour to emulate the printer becomes extremely interesting, particularly to those with an eye for display.

The devices used for tabular work vary on different machines, but generally the depression of a key or bar places the carriage at a position at which stops have been set for the insertion of the typewritten matter. This depression should be deep, so that the carriage arrives at the fixed stop at the one operation.

Estimating Width and Depth

An examination of the matter to be typed is the first essential, in order to gauge the maximum width and depth required for the complete work. Count the number of characters or characters and spaces in the widest line of each column or heading, and subtract the combined total from the number of spaces available in the width of the paper or the agreed width of the line of writing—Pica type allows ten letters to an inch, and Elite type allows twelve letters to an inch. The balance after this subtraction shows the amount of space that can be distributed as margins and white space between the columns. As regards depth of matter, there are six lines of single spacing to every inch, so that an estimate of the number of lines of writing and the line spaces to be left between the sections will enable the correct depth to be ascertained. The general rule is to place tabular work on the page so that the left and right margins are equal and the same amount of space is left at the top and bottom of the paper. On occasion, of course, this tabular work may be placed on a page with ordinary text and not form a distinct item.

Tabular Examples

An estimate of the space required for the following example will show the method of planning and provide excellent preliminary practice:

FEBRUARY

Sun	1	8	15	22
Mon	2	9	16	23
Tue	3	10	17	24
Wed	4	11	18	25
Thu	5	12	19	26
Fri	6	13	20	27
Sat	7	14	21	28

All the columns are narrow, and, to prevent undue space between each column, the width of the whole could be limited to, say, three inches (thirty Pica spaces). There are ten type spaces for the five columns (3, 1, 2, 2, 2). This leaves twenty spaces for division between the columns—five for each—and the remaining fifty spaces will permit of equal left and right margins

(25). The left-hand margin stop would therefore be set at 25, and tabular stops either set or placed in position (see page 18) for the columns at 33, 39, 46, and 53. There will be one depression of the space bar for the first two items of the third column, so as to bring them into correct relation to the others. The heading contains eight letters, and for centring should be indented eleven spaces from the margin stop—36 on the scale. Now set the margin and tabulator stops at the points mentioned and type this example.

When there are varying widths of line in a column it is advisable to insert leader dots to link up related items in other columns. These leader dots may be in a continuous line or in groups of two or three, as shown on p. 113.

A more difficult test will now receive attention. On p. 165 there is a handwritten draft which is to be typed across a sheet of quarto paper (80 spaces). There are five columns, and the total type area required is equivalent to sixty spaces. For margins and white space between the columns twenty spaces are available. An allocation in the following manner would give an effective display—the figures in brackets show how the twenty spaces have been distributed:

$$\left.\begin{array}{cccccccccccl} & 6 & & 18 & & 14 & & 12 & & 10 & & = 60 \\ (5) & & (2) & & (2) & & (3) & & (3) & & (5) & = 20 \end{array}\right\} 80$$

The allocation is often a matter of individual preference, and variations may be made that will be equally effective.

The main heading should be in capitals, and will require twenty-two spaces, including double space between the words. In the sub-heading there are thirty-five spaces. These two lines should be centred over the whole table; the first line will begin at 31 on the scale and the second line at 24. The left-hand margin should be set at 5, and the tabulator stops at 14, 34, 51, and 66. The use of the space bar will be necessary to secure accurate centring of the items.

Ruling in Ink

It is usual to rule up these tables in ink, and to do this accurately guide dots (light impressions of the full stop) can be inserted one line space above the first line of the column headings and one line space below the last line of the columns. There should be one space between the corner dots and the first or last letter of the end columns and dots should also be inserted between each column and also between the column heading and the columns of figures. When taken from the machine the rulings can be completed in ink. The points for ruling are shown in the worked example on p. 166.

Exercises

Exercise 61 contains a list of subjects, and for quarto paper width the allocation of spaces would be:

	12		11		11		13	
(9)		(5)		(5)		(5)		(9)

Set the margin at 9, and the tabulator stops at 26, 42, and 58. The heading requires eighteen spaces (two spaces between the words), and should begin at 31 on the scale.

Other exercises are included, and the same method should be followed when arranging for their preparation in tabular form.

SUPERANNUATION SCHEME

Table of benefits and contributions

Salary Class	Annual Salary or Wages	Annual pension payable from normal pension date for each complete year as a contributor in Salary Class	Employee's weekly contribution payable while in Salary Class	Life Assurance payable on death while in Salary Class
		£	£	£
A	not exceeding £156	1.00	·6	100
B	over £156 to £250	2.00	.12	150
C	over £250 to £350	3.00	.19	200
D	over £350 to £450	4.00	.25	250
E	over £450 to £550	5.00	.31	300
F	over £550 to £650	6.00	.37	400
G	over £650	7.00	.44	500

SUPERANNUATION SCHEME

Table of Benefits and Contributions

Salary Class	Annual Salary or wages	Annual pension payable from normal pension date for each complete year as a contributor in Salary Class	Employee's weekly contribution payable while in Salary Class	Life Assurance payable on death while in Salary Class
		£	£	£
A	not exceeding £156	1.00	.6	100
B	over £156 to £250	2.00	.12	150
C	over £250 to £350	3.00	.19	200
D	over £350 to £450	4.00	.25	250
E	over £450 to £550	5.00	.31	300
F	over £550 to £650	6.00	.37	400
G	over £650	7.00	.44	500

EXERCISE 61

List of Subjects

Accountancy	Dietetics	Mathematics	Printing
Advertising	Economics	Metallurgy	Refrigeration
Aeronautics	Elocution	Mineralogy	Salesmanship
Architecture	Engineering	Mining	Shipping
Arithmetic	English	Music	Shorthand
Banking	First-Aid	Needlework	Telegraphy
Book-Keeping	Geography	Optics	Telephony
Building	History	Pharmacy	Television
Calculations	Insurance	Photography	Theatre
Chemistry	Investment	Physics	Transport
Commerce	Journalism	Poetry	Typewriting

EXERCISE 62

"Electra" Machine
Quarterly Sales

Branch	Mch	June	Sept	Dec
Southampton	136	210	195	187
Portsmouth	125	167	154	170
Liverpool	103	141	139	126
Birmingham	214	230	179	223
Manchester	212	176	194	182
Leeds	317	265	276	284
Sheffield	284	314	237	330
Burnley	147	201	169	229
Middlesbrough	231	198	217	186
Cardiff	246	312	256	306
Swansea	193	224	184	219
Newport	231	189	209	196
Totals	2,439	2,627	2,409	2,638

EXERCISE 63

Arabic and Roman Numerals

Arabic	Roman small	Roman capitals	Arabic	Roman small	Roman capitals
1	i	I	15	xv	XV
2	ii	II	16	xvi	XVI
3	iii	III	17	xvii	XVII
4	iv	IV	18	xviii	XVIII
5	v	V	19	xix	XIX
6	vi	VI	20	xx	XX
7	vii	VII	30	xxx	XXX
8	viii	VIII	40	xl	XL
9	ix	IX	50	l	L
10	x	X	60	lx	LX
11	xi	XI	70	lxx	LXX
12	xii	XII	80	lxxx	LXXX
13	xiii	XIII	90	xc	XC
14	xiv	XIV	100	c	C

SECTION XVII

SPEED TESTS

IT may not be within the capacity of every typist to attain a championship rate, but the endeavour to effect an improvement will not be wasted; it will undoubtedly result in increased skill of operation, improved knowledge, and an enlarged vocabulary.

Regular practice on the exercises in the earlier sections should have secured a fair speed of operation. High speed will not be attained unless the touch system has been mastered; the eyes must be kept on the copy throughout the test. Other essentials for the attainment of speed are that there must be quick manipulation of the machine (particularly the carriage return), and that the typewriter must be kept in good condition.

Repetition Practice

One of the most helpful methods for increasing speed is repetition on straightforward printed matter, which should be typed and re-typed several times. The matter selected should be varied, and suitable pieces can be obtained from any book, magazine, or newspaper, but small print should be avoided. The repetition practice should be abandoned immediately there is any question of partial memorisation and a new piece should then be selected.

" Strokes " and Words

When the question of typewriting skill is being discussed it is usually in terms of ability to type at so many words a minute, but it is not generally understood that it is a measured word. It would not be reasonable for two lengthy words to have the same time value as two short words. Take, for example, " terminological inexactitude " for " an untruth." In the first rendering there are twenty-seven strokes or depressions of keys, including the space bar, and in the second there are only ten strokes or depressions.

The method of counting followed in typewriting contests and in the speed or accuracy tests set by the leading examining bodies is to give an average of five strokes for each word. Each depression, whether it be a character key or the space bar, counts as one stroke. No allowance is made for shift key work and indentation, but one stroke is added at the end of each line in lieu of space. Each space after a punctuation mark is allowed as a stroke. If a test containing 2,000 strokes is typed in ten minutes, the number of strokes is first divided by five to ascertain the number of words, and the result divided by the number of minutes to give the word rate for each minute. In this example the rate of typewriting would be 40 words a minute.

Deduction for Errors

For each error in a championship test there is a deduction of ten words (50 strokes). These errors may include irregular line spacing, lines too long or too short, paragraphs improperly indented, faulty spacing in relation to punctuation marks, imperfect impressions, transposed letters, words omitted or inserted, piling of letters at the end of a line, irregular left margin, erasures, etc.

Exercises

In the tests on pp. 173 to 181 each passage is arranged in accordance with examination procedure, the total number of words being given at the foot of the column indicating the line strokes. Should the typing end at an earlier " stroke " position, it will be an easy matter to find the actual speed at which the section has been typed—first divide the marginal number by five and then by the time taken to reach that point. The result of that division will give the number of words typed each minute.

Remember that, when attempting the tests, speed without accuracy is valueless. It is far better to have good quality than indifferent quantity, and an excellent motto to keep continually in mind is to " make haste slowly."

EXERCISE 64

	Strokes
Each age is an age of change, and most people are willing to change	68
with the times, giving up the old and taking what is new. There	133
are, however, a few who cannot or who will not change. At some	197
moment in their lives the willingness to consider new ideas and new	265
methods is lost, and from that time they look back, always back,	330
expressing a longing for the " good old days " and for the happi-	394
ness which for them is part of the past and which does not exist in	462
the present. It is, perhaps, in the country that the desire to keep	531
to the old order of things exists most strongly. Townspeople are	597
used to change: nothing is the same for very long. In the country	665
there is a more lasting quality about things. The little river that	734
runs across the field has run that way for years beyond number, and	802
is likely to continue to do so. The farm labourer would be very sur-	872
prised if the river were not there one day. But a town street is	938
always changing, and people will hardly turn their heads to look	1003
when workmen are pulling down some historic building.	1057
	(211 words)

EXERCISE 65

	Strokes
Long, long ago it was written that " Of making many books	57
there is no end." In those days books were so few that they were	123
quite beyond price. In these modern days, when to come to the	186
end of the book is merely to find that one is at the beginning of	252
another, the reader might add: " And of the reading of many	312
books there is no end." Once one has become a true reader one	375
cannot look upon books with anything but the deepest interest,	438
and, good though the book one is reading may be, there is always	503
the belief that the one waiting to be read will be of the most excep-	573
tional worth. This ever-present desire to pass on to the next book	641
results very often in our not getting out of a book all that it has	709
to offer of worth-while thought or information. The knowledge of	775
this fact causes us to remark, as we put down the book: " I must	840
read that again one of these days," but even as we say the words	906
we know that we shall not in all probability read it again, for	970
the next book is always calling us.	1006

This quick passing from book to book is no matter for surprise 1069
in view of the great numbers of books which are published. Books 1135
of every kind are at hand—books which simply tell a story; books 1203
which set out to teach us about some special subject; books which 1270
give an account of some outstanding event of war; books which 1333
open out for us the details of the life of this or that person. There 1404
are books about the past history of man, the history of nations, 1469
the history of industry; books which inform us of the conditions 1535
of life in other parts of the world; books relating to the political 1605
field; books about science and its relation to industry and to the 1673
life of the citizen; books by leaders of modern thought; books in 1741
our own language and books in other languages—books and books 1805
and books. Naturally, the opinions of the readers of these books 1871
differ as much as the books themselves differ. There are those who 1939
believe that modern writing has nothing worth-while to offer. 2001
Such people go back into the past for their reading material, and 2067
tell the world that whenever a new book is published they read 2130
an old one. 2141

(428 words)

EXERCISE 66

Strokes

The Works Engineer is responsible, through the Works Manager, 62
to the General Manager for the maintenance of all the machinery 126
and plant in the works, and for the personnel concerned there- 189
with. He is also concerned with the introduction of new equip- 253
ment to supplement or replace existing plant, and with the plan- 318
ning of the layout of the shops and the choice of design of the 382
actual machines. In some large works, however, there is a Plan- 447
ning Engineer who is responsible for the last-mentioned duties. 511
The Works Engineer must be able to adapt the plant to meet 570
the demands made by those in charge of actual production, or 631
by those individuals who have planned the works. It sometimes 694
happens, however, that the duties of planner and Works 749
Engineer are combined, and in such a case the official holding this 817
position would do well to invite suggestions from the different 881
repair sections regarding improved methods, both in keeping the 945
plant in the highest state of efficiency, and in the best and quickest 1016
ways of effecting repairs. 1043

It is found advantageous in a large works to employ one or more 1107
machine tool inspectors under the Works Engineer on these duties, 1173
one inspector undertaking also the duties of Safety Officer. 1234

The machine repair foreman must work in close co-operation 1293
with these engineers, reporting to them on the repairs necessary 1358
to machines, and indicating whether a machine is worn out, or 1420
whether it is fundamentally unsatisfactory. The inspectors are thus 1489
frequently able to provide reasons why a certain machine should 1553
be replaced, and indications are then made on the plant card in 1617
such cases. 1629

In most works today some kind of progress system is in opera- 1691
tion, and the Works Engineer should ensure that any breakdown 1753
of a machine should be immediately notified to the Progress or 1816
Planning Office, as it may be possible to make temporary arrange- 1881
ments to meet the emergency; whereas if the Progress Office were 1947
not promptly advised, dislocation of the programme would speedily 2013
ensue. 2019

(404 words)

EXERCISE 67

Strokes

Goods may be transported by land, sea or air. In this country 63
the greatest transportation of commodities in large bulk is by rail- 130
way, although a very considerable quantity of goods is now trans- 194
ported by fleets of large motor lorries for which trunk systems cover 264
the whole country. There is also a considerable coastwise traffic, 332
again mostly in large bulk. In this case the goods are carried in 399
small vessels known as " coasters " which voyage from one port to 463
another within the United Kingdom. A certain amount of freight 527
is still carried by barge on the inland canal system, but such traffic is 601
gradually decreasing. 624

The transport of goods in overseas transactions is mainly carried 690
out in ships, known as " freighters " which sail to all parts of the 757
world. For goods of high intrinsic value, or where speed is of great 827
importance, much use is now made of the air freight services, but 893
freight charges by air are still relatively high. 944

The packaging, dispatch and transport of goods, particularly 1005
where they are exported to destinations overseas, has now become a 1072

complicated procedure. Considerable knowledge and experience 1134
are required to ensure that the best routes are used and that the many 1205
formalities are complied with. Many of the larger organizations 1270
maintain their own shipping departments where the staff are specially 1340
trained in this kind of work. Traders who would find the mainten- 1405
ance of a special department unjustified will probably avail them- 1470
selves of the service of specialists who are known as forwarding 1535
agents. 1544

Since goods in transit are liable to loss or damage which might 1608
involve both the exporter and importer in heavy financial losses, 1674
these risks are covered by means of insurance which is also a special- 1743
ized business. 1759

Many firms now have their own delivery arrangements and main- 1819
tain fleets of motor lorries which cover a wide radius. This system 1888
has the advantage of being much quicker than transport by the goods 1956
or passenger services of the railways. Goods can be taken direct 2022
from the factory or warehouse of the supplier to the premises of the 2091
purchaser. 2101

(420 words)

EXERCISE 68

Strokes
The Stock Exchange, London, is not the only institution of its 63
kind in this country. It is by far the largest of the Stock Exchanges, 135
and the volume of each day's trading stamps it at once as quite 199
the most important. London's age and membership give it the 260
premier position, and its unique system of Jobbers, whereby a 322
more free market exists than in other Exchanges, makes it the 384
centre to which the bulk of investment and speculative business 448
naturally flows. It follows that it is often more convenient for a 516
client who lives, say, in Liverpool to call and consult his Broker 583
there, when discussion on financial matters can freely take place, 650
than to be compelled to enter into voluminous correspondence 711
with a Broker whom he does not know. It is far more satisfactory 777
for the London Broker also, as that personal knowledge and touch 842
so necessary in business must of necessity be lacking under such 907
circumstances. 922

These conditions have resulted in the opening up from time to 984
time of Stock Exchanges in many of the large cities; several towns of 1055
importance also have their own representative institutions. Smaller 1124
localities can also be recognised as properly constituted for officially 1197
conducting Stock Exchange business. The large institutions, 1258
situated as near as Birmingham and as remote as Belfast, are known 1325
as the Provincial Exchanges. 1354

The Provincial Exchanges, many of them in the heart of the 1413
large industrial areas, transact among their own Members an 1473
important business, and contribute to London a steady stream of 1537
orders. These orders represent business that it is found impossible 1606
to execute in the Provincial Exchanges. As far as is practicable, 1673
clients' orders are carried out in the local Exchange to which a 1738
Stockbroker belongs, the Member there dealing with a fellow- 1799
Member. When he is unable so to deal the order is passed through 1865
to London, or to another Stock Exchange in the Provinces. 1922

(384 words)

SECTION XVIII

MISCELLANEOUS TYPEWRITTEN EXAMPLES

In this section various typewritten examples are reproduced, and they provide additional copying practice. Most documents like these are legal ones. Those connected with commercial transactions are often partially printed, with blanks to be completed by the typist. This applies particularly to banking, insurance, and shipping business, but legal instruments are likely to be more individual in character, and have therefore to be typed in full.

All the important words are typed in capitals or spaced capitals. The documents may be drafted, and afterwards completed on different papers, the standard sizes used in most offices being:

	Width	*Length*
A4 . . .	8·3″	11·7″
A5 . . .	8·3″	5·8″

International Paper Sizes A4 and A5 have now taken over from the standard quarto (8″ × 10″) and foolscap (8″ × 13″). Quarto and foolscap papers were those most commonly used for documents of all descriptions. Quarto paper (the same width as foolscap) has been used for the examples given, to permit of photographic reproduction within the limited area of the page. The layout across the page is the same for all papers, the difference being in depth only. For legal documents paper with the main headings printed in German text type, and with rules margins, can be obtained from law stationers, but, when plain paper is used, the headings are typed in display form. Ink ruling is the general practice for portions underlined, but when this is very limited, the underscore can be used. Abbreviations and words divided at line ends may be included in the drafts, but not in the engrossments or final copies prepared for completion.

When dealing with tabular work, the procedure for the setting of margin and tabulator stops was explained, and in the items which follow the stops named are those which were set when the originals of the type-written examples were prepared. There may be slight variations in actual practice, but in the main they are representative.

Abstract of Title

An abstract of title consists of a summary of the contents of deeds which establish the ownership of specified property. It may be typed in double-line spacing on foolscap or in treble-line spacing on brief paper, and in the example on p. 188 the general arrangement is shown for a foolscap layout (margin 5; indented portions 20, 25, 30, and 40), with the heading in spaced capitals. For brief paper the scale points would be adjusted to give a bolder display (margin 15; other stops at 30, 40, 50, and 65).

Affidavit

Foolscap paper is used for this declaration given on oath before a commissioner for oaths or other recognised authority. This document should be typed in double-line spacing, and the headings arranged in capitals, with the names of the parties centred, as shown in the reproduction on p. 190. The left margin stop is set at 15 on the scale, and the paragraphs indented five spaces.

Agreement

The example on p. 192 is of a Tenancy Agreement, and the general arrangement is simple—foolscap paper, with a left-hand margin of 15 and indentations of five spaces for each paragraph. The capitalisation should be noted, and ample space should be left for the signatures of the parties and the witnesses to those signatures.

Conveyance

In this example on p. 196 the layout follows somewhat the Agreement, except that the matter has a continuous run and not paragraph form. As there is a fair amount of underlining, this should be done in ink. Note the capitalisation, and set the margin stops at 10 and 75.

Dramatic Work

This will contain title-page, synopsis of acts and scenery, cast and characters, followed by the spoken parts, and it is a portion of this last-named part that is reproduced. Quarto or A4 paper is used; the first portions require careful centring and display, but the play itself presents little difficulty. Names of speakers are placed alongside their respective parts. All descriptive words not spoken are underlined. The example on p. 200 is from a short play by L. du Garde Peach, and the title-page of the book from which it is taken was used for the display on p. 159.

Specification

A specification contains particulars of work to be performed. Foolscap paper is generally used, and the sub-headings are typed in the margin, for quick reference. Double or single-line spacing is permissible, according to length or preference, and the paragraph indentations are five spaces from a margin set at 15 on the scale, as shown in the example on p. 202.

Statutory Declaration

Made in accordance with the Statutory Declarations Act, 1835, this document is typed on foolscap paper with double-line spacing. Set the margin at 15 on the scale and indentations five spaces from this margin. The heading and the name of the person making the declaration should be typed in capitals. The example for this document appears on p. 204.

Will

A Will is an instrument providing for the distribution or administration of property after the death of the testator. Foolscap paper is used and the document typed in double-line spacing. The opening words and the first word of each section are in capitals, as shown in the specimen on p. 206. The left-hand margin may be set at 10, and the attestation clause at 5, so as to ensure that there is ample space for the signature of the testator and the witnesses.

Endorsements

The endorsement is placed on the back of the document, and should contain the date, names of the parties, a brief description of the contents, and the name of the solicitors by whom the document has been prepared.

Foolscap paper can be folded into four, or lengthwise into two. When folding into four, place the paper face upwards, and fold into two by placing the bottom edge level with the top edge and creasing flat; then place the folded edge with the open edges and crease again. The endorsement should be on the uppermost side when folded. For a lengthwise fold, place the paper face upwards and fold the left edge over the right edge until the two edges meet, and then crease. The endorsement should be on the right half of the crease on the last sheet.

Two examples are given on p. 187; they are the endorsements required for the specimen Abstract of Title and the Agreement.

Dated 19--	Dated 19--
WILLIAM FREDERICK RICHARDSON	
and	ABSTRACT OF TITLE
CHARLES HENRY SIMPSON	of
-------------	HENRY JOHN REYNOLDS
	to
A G R E E M E N T	Ivydene, Grove Road Walton, Essex
for	-------------
T E N A N C Y	

Cunningham, Jones & Co. Imperial Buildings ROMFORD	William Drake & Co. 419 Union Street BRIGHTON

Specimen layout for Endorsements (see p. 185).

Specimen layout for an Abstract of Title (see p. 183).

A B S T R A C T   O F   T I T L E

--------- of ---------

HENRY JOHN REYNOLDS to freehold
premises known as "Ivydene" Grove
Road Walton in the County of Essex

1st June, 19-- BY CONVEYANCE of this date between WILLIAM FISH of 10 Grange Avenue Deal in the County of Kent Merchant (thereinafter called the vendor) of the one part and HENRY JOHN REYNOLDS of 41 Horsham Road Worthing in the County of Sussex Solicitor (thereinafter called the purchaser) of the other part

RECITING the seisin of the vendor in fee simple

AND RECITING agreement for sale at the price of

£950

<u>IT IS WITNESSED</u> that in pursuance of the said agreement and in consideration of £950 paid (the receipt etc) the vendor thereby granted and conveyed unto the purchaser his heirs and assigns

<u>ALL THAT</u> piece of land situate on the West side of Grove Road Walton in the County of Essex containing in front thereof abutting on the said road 42 feet or thereabouts, and measuring from front to rear on the North side thereof 105 feet or thereabouts and on the South side thereof 136 feet or thereabouts which said piece of land with the dimensions, etc.

Specimen layout for an Affidavit (*see p. 183*).

IN THE HIGH COURT OF JUSTICE 19-- S. No. 1212

QUEEN'S BENCH DIVISION

B E T W E E N CHARLES STONEHAM

Plaintiff

and

JOHN BAX and DAVID CROSS

Defendants

I, CHARLES STONEHAM, of 453 Salisbury Road, Worthing, in the County of Sussex, the abovenamed Plaintiff, make oath and say as follows:-

1. The abovenamed Defendants John Bax and David Cross are and were at the date of the issue of the Writ of Summons in

this Action justly and truly indebted to me in the moneys claimed by the endorsement of the Writ of Summons herein.

2. Full particulars of such indebtedness appear by the said endorsement and such particulars are true.

3. In my belief the Defendants have no Defence to this Action and appearance has only been entered for the purpose of delay.

SWORN at ....)
in the County of Sussex, this)
..... day of 19--   )

Before me,

A Commissioner for Oaths

Specimen layout for an Agreement (*see p. 184*).

A N A G R E E M E N T made the

One thousand nine hundred and B E T W E E N

WILLIAM FREDERICK RICHARDSON of 134 Evanston Road Brentwood in the County of Essex Electrical Engineer (hereinafter called "the Landlord") of the one part and CHARLES HENRY SIMPSON of 149 Upper Colchester Terrace Chelmsford in the said County Confectioner (hereinafter called "the Tenant") of the other part W H E R E B Y it is agreed as follows:

1. The Landlord shall let and the Tenant shall take ALL THAT messuage or dwellinghouse situate and known as No. 96 Palmerston Avenue Folkestone in the County of Kent for a term of three years from the date hereof at the yearly rent of Two hundred pounds payable in four equal quarterly

instalments on the usual quarter days the first of such payments to be made on the twenty-fourth day of June next.

2. The Tenant shall pay all rates taxes and assessments payable by the Tenant or occupier in respect of the premises during the tenancy.

3. The Tenant shall keep all internal fixtures and fittings belonging to the premises in good and sufficient repair during the tenancy and deliver up the same in such repair at the end thereof reasonable wear and tear and damage by fire excepted.

4. The Tenant shall not assign underlet or part with the possession of the premises or any part thereof without the previous consent in writing of the Landlord.

5. The Landlord shall insure the premises against fire and apply any insurance money in reinstating the damaged premises.

6. The Landlord agrees that the Tenant paying the said rent and observing the conditions herein contained shall quietly hold and enjoy the premises without any lawful interruption by the Landlord or any person lawfully claiming under him.

7. If any rent shall be in arrear for fifteen days whether legally demanded or not or there shall be any breach by the Tenant of the conditions herein contained or if the Tenant shall become bankrupt then and in any such case the Landlord may re-enter upon the said premises or any part

thereof in the name of the whole and thereupon the tenancy shall determine.

IN WITNESS whereof the parties hereto have hereunto set their hands the day and year first above written.

SIGNED by the said William Frederick)
Richardson in the presence of)

SIGNED by the said Charles Henry)
Simpson in the presence of)

Specimen layout for a Conveyance (see p. 184).

<u>T H I S C O N V E Y A N C E</u> made the day of
One thousand nine hundred and <u>B E T W E E N</u> HENRY
FOX of Elm House Chigwell in the County of Essex Gentleman
(hereinafter called the Vendor) of the one part and ADELAIDE
BAKER of Ivydene Northwood Road Dover in the County of Kent
Widow (hereinafter called the Purchaser) of the other part
<u>WHEREAS</u> the Vendor is seised in fee simple in possession free
from incumbrances of the property hereinafter described and
has agreed with the Purchaser for the sale to her for the sum
of Two thousand pounds of the said property in fee simple in
possession <u>NOW THIS DEED WITNESSETH</u> that in pursuance of the
said agreement and in consideration of the sum of Two thousand
pounds paid by the Purchaser to the Vendor (the receipt of

which sum the Vendor hereby acknowledges) the Vendor as Beneficial Owner doth hereby <u>CONVEY</u> unto the Purchaser <u>ALL THAT</u> piece or parcel of land situate in the parish of Chigwell in the County of Essex on the South side of a road there called Manse End and having a frontage thereto of two hundred feet or thereabouts and abutting on the East to land belonging to the Purchaser and on the South and West to land belonging to the Vendor <u>ALL WHICH</u> said piece of land is more particularly delineated with the dimensions and abuttals thereof on the plan drawn in the margin of these presents and thereon coloured pink and which said piece or parcel of land Numbered 461 and delineated and coloured blue on the plan drawn on a certain Deed of Conveyance dated the 17th day of June 19-- and made between John Brown of the one part and the Vendor of the other part TO HOLD the same unto and to the use of the Purchaser in fee simple AND the Vendor hereby acknowledges the right of the Purchaser to production of the documents mentioned in the Schedule hereto (the possession of which is retained by the Vendor) and to delivery of copies thereof AND hereby undertakes with the Purchaser for the safe custody of the same documents IN WITNESS whereof the parties to these presents have hereunto set their hands and seals the day and year first above written

THE SCHEDULE above referred to

10th May, 1896 CONVEYANCE made between Francis Woodman
of the first part Frederick Bond of the

	second part and John Redman of the third part.
10th May, 1896	COVENANT for production of deeds made between Francis Woodman of the first part Frederick Bond of the second part and John Redman of the third part.
17th June, 1926	CONVEYANCE made between John Brown of the one part and Henry Fox of the other part.

SIGNED SEALED and DELIVERED by)
the abovenamed HENRY FOX in the)
presence of)

Specimen layout of section of a Play (see p. 184).

S I R   L A U N C E L O T

O F   T H E   L A K E

----------oOo----------

PEOPLE IN THE PLAY

Sir Caradoc	Servant
Sir Launcelot	Merlin
Queen Morgan le Fay	

A room in SIR CARADOC'S castle with a very heavy-looking door. There is no window.

At a table with fruit, wine, etc., QUEEN MORGAN LE FAY is sitting with SIR CARADOC. A SERVANT pours wine for them.

CARADOC.   Leave us!

(The SERVANT goes out.)

Now you may speak freely.

MORGAN.   I will. You, Sir Caradoc, have no love for Arthur, my brother.

CARADOC. I have no more love for him than you.

MORGAN. I hate him! But for him - and Merlin, with his magic arts - my husband, King Lot, would have been overlord of Britain. Instead of which he has to do homage to him - to Arthur!

CARADOC. True.

MORGAN. It is time that Arthur, with his Round Table of knights, was exterminated as one stamps out a nest of scorpions.

CARADOC. I should be happy to see it.

MORGAN. You shall be happy.

CARADOC. Arthur is strong, the strongest king in Britain. All others are lesser and tributary to him.

MORGAN. Arthur is stronger than any single king, but not stronger than all. Together, they could overwhelm him and his knights.

Specimen layout of a Specification (*see p. 185*).

S P E C I F I C A T I O N of work required to be done in the erection of a villa at Epping for Mr. Frank Jones, in accordance with Drawings prepared by Mr. John Dean of 10 High Road, Epping, the Architect referred to in this specification.

10th May, 19--

PRELIMINARY and GENERAL

NOTICES AND FEES — Give all requisite notices to the Local and other Authorities, obtain all licences, and pay all fees.

SETTING-OUT — The Contractor is to set out the whole of the works in accordance with the plans; and he will be responsible for the correctness of the setting-out, and is to amend the same if it shall be found by the Architect to be incorrect.

DIMENSIONS ON DRAWINGS

Figured dimensions are, in all cases, to be taken in preference to scale, and the large scale details to be followed in preference to small scale general drawings. In the event of any apparent discrepancy between the drawings or between the drawings and this specification, the Contractor is to ask for an explanation from the Architect before proceeding.

SCAFFOLDING

The Contractor is to supply all scaffolding and plant required for the works.

WATER AND LIGHTING

Pay all charges for water and lighting required during the erection of the building.

Specimen Layout of a Statutory Declaration (*see p. 185*).

STATUTORY DECLARATION

I GEORGE HERBERT BROWN of 437 Church Road Colchester in the County of Essex Solicitor do solemnly and sincerely DECLARE that:

1. I am the registered proprietor or holder of the shares numbered 101 to 350 both inclusive of The Rex Manufacturing Company Limited and in respect of such shares the said Company issued to me share certificate No. 75.

2. I have made and caused to be made diligent search and inquiry for the said share certificate but I have been unable to find the same and I verily believe that the said share certificate has been lost mislaid or destroyed.

3. The said share certificate has not been deposited or

agreed to be deposited as security with any person firm or corporation either by myself or to the best of my knowledge by any other person or persons and I am the only person entitled to the said shares and to receive a new certificate in lieu of the certificate so lost mislaid or destroyed.

AND I make this solemn declaration conscientiously believing the same to be true and by virtue of the provisions of the Statutory Declarations Act 1835.

DECLARED at ....)
in the County of Essex this ....)
day of .... 19--)

Before me,

A Commissioner for Oaths

Specimen layout of a Will (*see p. 185*).

<u>THIS IS THE LAST WILL AND TESTAMENT</u> of me ALBERT BETHELL of 56 Garner Road St. Albans in the County of Hertfordshire Civil Servant ----------------------------------

I REVOKE all testamentary writings heretofore made by me.---

I DEVISE all the real estate to which I shall be entitled at the time of my death unto and to the use of my wife ALICE BETHELL for her life without impeachment of waste and after her decease to the use of my son RICHARD BETHELL absolutely.------------------------------

I BEQUEATH all the chattels real and personal estate to which I shall be entitled at the time of my death unto my said wife and son upon trust to sell and convert the same into money and therefrom to pay my debts and funeral and testamentary expenses and a legacy of Five hundred pounds to my said wife and to invest the clear residue thereof upon trust to permit my said wife to receive the income of the said investments during her life and after her death to transfer the capital thereof to my said son.

I APPOINT my said wife and my said son Executors of this my Will.---

IN WITNESS whereof I have hereunto set my hand this ...... day of .... One thousand nine hundred and ....

SIGNED by ALBERT BETHELL the testator)
in the presence of us present at the)
same time who in his presence and at)
his request and in the presence of)
each other have hereunto subscribed)
our names as witnesses)
)
)

SECTION XIX

REFERENCE BOOKS

WORKS of reference are indispensable for every typist, and their value cannot be over-emphasised. There are many occasions, both in private and in business life, when specialist information is urgently required. The main points to be borne in mind are: (1) knowing where to look; (2) knowing how to look; and (3) knowing how to abstract information correctly and quickly.

When the information is being sought in the reference room of a public library, the librarian can often suggest the most likely sources for securing that information. There must be the ability to use the books skilfully, dexterity in the use of an alphabetical index, and quickness to appreciate all the headings under which a particular subject may be mentioned. A perusal of any reference book will be enough to make one acquainted with the alphabetical system of classification and with the use of cross-references.

In the modern public library the publications available generally include not only dictionaries, encyclopædias, directories, and annuals of every description, but all important Government handbooks, periodicals, and up-to-date information of all kinds.

Typists connected with the various trades and professions will no doubt be able to peruse the specialist journals subscribed for by their principals, and the following details concern a small selection of reference books which collectively contain a mine of information. Some of them may not be part of the office equipment, but they are all of special interest, and can be consulted in most libraries.

An *English Dictionary* is an essential part of the typist's equipment. Dictionaries are probably consulted more than any other book of reference; they usually give the spelling, pronunciation, derivation, and meaning of words. Many of them contain appendices with lists of foreign words, pronunciation of proper names, weights and measures, etc. Always look up unknown words and note the definitions and uses of those words.

There are *Encyclopædias* which provide information on a very large variety of subjects in a compact and convenient form. They may give reliable statistical and descriptive material concerning governments, peoples, individuals, and trading relations, or contain specialised technical information.

Another useful and interesting volume is the *Writers' and Artists' Year Book*, a directory for writers, journalists, artists, playwrights, writers for the films and broadcasting, photographers, designers, and composers. The book includes an up-to-date list of English, Canadian, Australian, New Zealand, and South African publishers and periodicals and their requirements and rates of payment, and much information regarding copyright, agreements, serial rights, etc.

The qualifications, appointments, publications, etc., of about 40,000 British men and women in the public eye are given in the concise biographies contained in that well-known work *Who's Who*.

In *Whitaker's Almanack* there will be found an account of the astronomical and other phenomena and a vast amount of information respecting the government, finance, population, commerce, and general statistics of the various nations of the world, with an index containing 35,000 references. This popular work of reference is issued annually.

A work of exceptional interest to all concerned with typewriters and typewriting is *The Dictionary of Typewriting*. Every branch of the subject is covered; modern typewriting devices are dealt with; hints on operation are given, and there are articles on all matters connected with the subject.

An *Atlas* and *Gazetteer* will provide the correct spelling and location of places about which one may have only a vague idea; it is a profitable habit to refer to them constantly, for in addition to showing their place on the map, they usually furnish such details as climate, population, products, etc.

There are in addition many *Ready Reckoners*, *Discount and Interest Tables*, and another essential reference book is the *Post Office Guide*. This list of books could be considerably extended, but those referred to here are extremely useful in most business houses.

SECTION XX

ABBREVIATIONS

TIME-SAVING devices are essential in business, and one which requires careful attention is the use of abbreviations. They are shortened forms of words and phrases, and have become established by common usage. In many cases they consist of initials only.

The use of the full stop is usual after a recognised abbreviation; there are, however, certain signs and symbols which do not need the full stop, e.g. the £ sign, the ampersand (&), @ (at), and IOU (I owe you).

In the following list examples of approved longhand and legal abbreviations have been included.

A

@, at; for; to; from.
A1, "first class"; first class (at Lloyd's).
A/A., articles of association.
A.A., Automobile Association.
a.a., always afloat (chartering).
A.A.A., Amateur Athletic Association.
A.A.G., Assistant-Adjutant-General.
a.a.r., against all risks.
A.B., Able-bodied Seaman.
A/B, Limited Company (Swedish).
Abp., Archbishop.
abr., abridged, abridgment.
abstt. (legal), abstract.
abt., about.
ac., acre.
a.c., alternating current.
A/c or acct., account.
A/C, account current.
A.C.A., Associate, Institute of Chartered Accountants.
acc., acceptance, accepted.
accrdg., according.
A.C.C.S., Associate, Corporation of Certified Secretaries.
acct., account.
acct., accountant.
ackgt., acknowledgment.
acknl. (legal), acknowledge.
A.D., *anno Domini* (in the year of our Lord).
a/d, after date.
A.D.C., Aide-de-camp.
adjn., adjourn.
adjnd., adjourned.
adjmt., adjournment.
adjudn. (legal), adjudication.
ad lib., *ad libitum* (at pleasure).
Adm., Admiral.
admix. (legal), administratrix.
admor. (legal), administrator.
Admy., Admiralty.
ads. or **adverts.**, advertisements.
adv. advice.
ad val., *ad valorem* (at value).
advg. (legal), advising.
advt., advertisement.

afft. (legal), affidavit.
afsd. (legal), aforesaid.
aftn., afternoon.
A.-G., Attorney-General, Agent-General, Adjutant-General.
a.g.b., any good brand.
agn., again.
agrt. (legal), agreement.
agst., against.
agt., agent.
a.h., after hatch (shipping).
Ald., Alderman.
alteron. (legal), alteration.
altho., although.
a.m., *ante meridiem* (before mid-day).
amendt. (legal), amendment.
amgst., amongst.
amt., amount.
anny. (legal), annuity.
anon., anonymous.
anr., another.
ans., answer.
A/o., account of.
A/o, and/or.
A.P., additional premium (insurance).
app., appendix.
applon. (legal), application.
appro., approval.
approx., approximate.
apptd. (legal), appointed.
appurts. (legal), appurtenances.
a/r, all risks (marine insurance).
A.A.R., against all risks.
arr., arrive, arrival.
arrangt. (legal), arrangement.
A/S, Account Sales; Joint-Stock Co., Ltd. (Norwegian).
A/s, at sight; after sight; alongside (chartering).
Assn., Association.
assns. (legal), assigns.
asst., assistant.
attdce., attendance.
attg. (legal), attending.
attestn. (legal), attestation.
atty. (legal), attorney.
ats. (legal), at the suit of.
authy. (legal), authority.
av., average.
av. or avoir, or avdp., avoirdupois.
a/v, *ad valorem* (according to value).
avge., average.

B

B.A., Bachelor of Arts.
back., backwardation (Stock Exchange).
bal., balance.
bar., barrel.
B.B., Bill Book; an Inwards Clearance certificate (shipping).
B.Ch., Bachelor of Surgery.
B/D., bank draft; bills discounted.
b/d, brought down.
bd., bond; bound; board.
bdle., bundle.
bdth., breadth.
B/E, bill of exchange; bill of entry (customs).
befe. (legal), before.
bequed. (legal), bequeathed.
B. of E., Bank of England.
bf. (legal), brief.
b/f, brought forward.
B.G., Birmingham gauge.
B/H, Bordeaux Hamburg range.
B.H.P. or b.h.p., brake horse-power.
bk., bank; book; backwardation.
bkcy. (legal), bankruptcy.
bkpt., bankrupt.
B.L., bill of lading.
bl., bale; barrel.
bldg., building.
blk., black.
B.Mus., Bachelor of Music.
bn., been.
B.N., bank note.
B.O., Board's Orders (customs); branch office.
B.O.D., buyer's option to double.
B/P, bill payable.
B.P., British Pharmacopœia.
B.P.B., Bank Post Bill.

b.p., below proof.
bque., barque.
B.R., British Railways.
B/R, bill receivable; Bordeaux or Rouen (grain trade).
brev., brevet (patent).
brl., barrel.
B/S, bill of sale; bill of store.
b/s, bags; bales.
B.Sc., Bachelor of Science.
bsh. or **bus.**, bushel.
B/St., bill of sight.
b.t., berth terms.
Bt., Baronet.
B.Th.U., British Thermal Unit.
btwn., between.
B.W.G., Birmingham Wire Gauge.
bx(s)., **box(es)**.

C

C., centigrade.
C.A., Chartered Accountant (Scotland); County Alderman.
C/A, Capital Account; Commercial Agent.
c., case.
C. & F., Cost and Freight.
Cantab., of Cambridge.
cat., catalogue.
C.C., County Council; continuation clause (insurance).
c.c., cubic centimetre.
c/d, carried down.
C.D., commercial dock.
C. & D., collected and delivered (Railway rates).
c.d. or **cum div.**, cum dividend (with the dividend).
C/E, Customs Entry.
C.E., Civil Engineer.
C/E Charges, Captain's Entry Charges.
cert., certificate.
cert. inv., certified invoice.
c/f, carried forward.
c.f., cubic feet.
cf., compare.
C.F.I., same as C.I.F.
C.f.o., Coast for orders (for discharging—chartering).
cg., centigramme.
cge., carriage.
C.H., Custom House; Clearing House; Companion of Honour.
ch., chapter.
Ch.D., Chancery Division.
ch. fwd., charges forward.
chge. (legal), charge.
ch. ppd., charges prepaid.
chq., cheque.
C.I., Channel Isles.
C.I.F. (sif.), Cost, Insurance and Freight.
C.I.F. & C., Cost, Insurance, Freight and Commission.
C.I.F.C. & E., Cost, Insurance, Freight, Commission and Exchange.
C.I.F. & C. & S., Cost, Insurance, Freight, and Commission and Seizure.
C.I.F.C. & I., Cost, Insurance, Freight, Commission and Interest.
circs., circumstances.
ck., cask.
cl., centilitre; clause; class.
cld., cleared (goods, shipping).
c/m, call of more (Stock Exchange).
cm., centimetre.
cml., commercial.
C/N or **C/note**, credit note; consignment note.
Co., Company; County.
co. (legal), copy.
C/O, Cash Order (banking).
c/o, care of.
C/O, certificate of origin.
co. claim (legal), counterclaim.
C.O.D., cash on delivery.
codl. (legal), codicil.
Col. (legal), Counsel.
collr., collector.
comdg., commanding.
comee., committee.
commr. (legal), Commissioner.
compenson. (legal), compensation.

concerng. (legal), concerning.
confce., conference.
consgt., consignment.
considn., consideration.
conson. (legal), consideration.
consultn. (legal), consultation.
Consve., Conservative.
contce. (legal), continuance.
contd. (legal), contained.
contg., containing.
contt. (legal), contract.
convce. (legal), conveyance.
co. pt. (legal), counterpart.
coy., company.
C/P, Charter Party.
cp., compare.
c.p., candle-power.
C.p.d., Charterers pay dues.
C.R., Company's Risk (Railway rates).
C.r.v., Cloth, on rollers, and varnished (maps, etc.).
C/S, Colliery screened (coal trade).
C.S., Clerk to the Signet; Common Sergeant.
C/s, cases.
csk., cask.
C.T.L., constructive total loss.
cum div., with the dividend.
Cum. Pref., Cumulative Preference.
cur., curt., currt., current.
C.W.C., County whence consigned (customs term).
C.w.o., cash with order.
cwt., hundredweight = 112 lb.

D

D/A, documents against acceptance; documents attached; discharge afloat (chartering); deposit account.
d. and b., deals and boards (shipping).
daurs. (legal), daughters.
D.B., Day Book.
D.B.B., deals, battens and boards (shipping).
dbk., drawback.
D.C., Detention Clause (Marine Insurance).
D/C, Deviation Clause (Marine Insurance).
d.c., direct current.
D/D, demand draft; deposited on drawback.
d/d, days after date; delivered docks.
dd., delivered.
dd./s, delivered sound (grain trade).
ddt., deduct.
D.D. and Shpg., dock dues and shipping.
dec., decrease.
deced. (legal), deceased.
declon. (legal), declaration.
deft., defendant.
defce. (legal), defence.
def., deferred.
deg., degree.
deld. (legal), delivered.
del., delete (strike out).
deposn. (legal), deposition.
dept., department.
descdt. (legal), descendant.
descron. (legal), description.
d.f., dead freight.
dft., draft.
dg., decigram.
diam., diameter.
diffce., difference.
diffy., difficulty.
diron. (legal), direction.
dis., discount.
dischge. (legal), discharge.
discron. (legal), discretion.
Dist., district.
Div., division.
div. or **divd.**, dividend.
Dk., dock.
dk., dark.
D.L., Deputy-Lieutenant.
D.Litt. or **D.Lit.**, Doctor of Letters.
D.L.O., Dead Letter Office.
d.l.o., dispatch loading only.
D.Mus. or **Mus.D.**, Doctor of Music.
D/N, debit note.

D/O, delivery order.
doct. (legal), document.
dols., dollars.
doz., dozen.
D/P, documents against payment; duty paid.
D.Ph., or D.Phil., Doctor of Philosophy.
Dr., debtor; drawer; doctor.
dr., drachma; dram; drams.
D/R, deposit receipt (banking).
drg. (legal), drawing.
drs. (legal), debtors.
d/s., days after sight.
D.Sc., Doctor of Science.
D.V., *deo volente* (God willing).
D/W, dock warrant.
D.w., dead weight.
Dwg. ho. (legal), dwelling house.
dwt., pennyweight.
Dy. or D/y or dely., delivery.

E

Ea., each.
E. & O.E., errors and omissions excepted.
easmt. (legal), easement.
Ebor, of York.
ed., edition; editor.
E.E., errors excepted.
Edin., Edinburgh.
e.g., for example.
E.I., East Indies.
E/I, Endorsement irregular (banking).
e.m.f., electromotive force.
enc. or enclo., enclosure.
ency., encyclopædia.
entd., entered.
eq., equivalent.
E.R. *Elizabeth Regina* (Queen Elizabeth).
E. Region, Eastern Region.
especly., especially.
estabt., establishment.
este. (legal), estate.
et seq., *et sequentia* (and the following).
evce. (legal), evidence.
ex., examined; exchange; Exchequer Reports (law); executed; out of; without.
ex all, without any dividends, rights, etc.
exam., examination.
exch., exchange; exchequer.
ex cp., ex (without) coupon.
exd., examined.
ex cont., from contract.
ex div., without the dividend.
ex in., without the interest.
ex new, without the new shares.
exors. (legal), executors.
ex pte. (legal), *ex parte*.
exs., expenses.

F

f., for; feet; folio; franc.
f.a.a., free of all average.
fac., facsimile.
Fahr., Fahrenheit.
f.a.q., fair average quality; free alongside quay.
f.a.s., free alongside ship.
F.C. & S., free of capture and seizure (shipping).
fco., franco (free).
f. co. (legal), fair copy.
fcp. or fcap., foolscap.
f.c.s., free of capture and seizure.
F.D., Defender of the Faith.
F/d, free docks; free dispatch.
F. & D., freight and demurrage.
ff., folios.
f.f.a., free from alongside.
f.g.a., free of general average.
fgn., foreign.
f.h., fore hatch.
f.i.b., free into bunkers; free into barge.
f.i.o., free in and out.
fir., firkin.
f.i.t., free of income tax.
fl., florin.
fm., from.
fm., fathom.
fo. or fol., folio.
F/o., for orders; full out terms (grain trade).
F.O., firm offer; Foreign Office.

f.o.b., free on board.
f.o.c., free of charge.
folg., following.
f.o.q., free on quay.
For., foreign.
f.o.r., free on rail.
f.o.r.t., full out Rye terms (grain trade).
forwd., forward.
f.o.s., free on ship; free on steamer.
f.o.t., free on trucks.
f.o.w., first open water; free on wagons.
F/P, Fire Policy.
f.p., fully paid.
f.p.a., free of particular average.
Fr., franc; French; Father.
f.r., freight release.
freehd. (legal), freehold.
frt. fwd., freight forward.
frt. ppd., freight prepaid.
ft., foot; feet.
F.T., Full terms.
fthm., fathom.
f.t.w., Free Trade Wharf.
fur., furlong.
fwd., forward.

G

g., gauge; gramme.
G.A., general average (marine insurance).
gall(s)., gallon(s).
gaz., gazette.
g.b.o., goods in bad order.
genl., general.
genly., generally.
G. gr., great gross. (144 doz.).
gl., gill.
G.L.C., Greater London Council.
G.M., Good Middling.
g.m.b., good merchantable brand.
g.m.q., good merchantable quality.
G.M.T., Greenwich Mean Time.
g.o.b., good ordinary brand.
Gov., Governor.
Govt., Government.
G.P.O., General Post Office.
G.R., *Georgius Rex* (King George).
Gr., grain; gross; Greek.
G.R.C., General Railway Classification (of goods).
grs., grains.
gs., guineas.
gr. wt., gross weight.
G.v., *Grande vitesse* (quick goods train).

H

h., have.
H.A. or D., Havre, Antwerp or Dunkirk.
Hants, Hampshire.
H.B.M., Her Britannic Majesty.
H/C, held covered.
H.E., His Eminence; His Excellency.
hf. bd., half bound.
hf. cf., half calf.
H.H., His Holiness; His Highness.
hhd., hogshead.
H.I.M., His (or Her) Imperial Majesty.
H.M.C., His (or Her) Majesty's Customs.
H.M.I., Her Majesty's Inspector.
H.M.S.O., Her Majesty's Stationery Office.
howr. (legal), however.
H.P., half pay; high pressure; horse-power; hire-purchase.
H.P.N., horse-power nominal.
h.r., high resistance.
H.R.H., His (or Her) Royal Highness.
hr(s)., hour(s).
hrar. (legal), hereafter.
hrnar. (legal), hereinafter.
hrnbfre., hereinbefore.
hrs. (legal), heirs.
H.T., half-time survey (shipping); high tension.
htofore. (legal), heretofore.
H.W.M., High Water Mark.
hyd., hydrostatics.
hydr., hydraulic.

I

ib., ibid., ibidem, in the same place.
id., idem, the same.
i.e., that is.
I/F, insufficient funds (banking).
I.H.P., indicated horse-power.
I/I, indorsement irregular (banking).
immdly., immediately.
imp., Imperial.
impce. (legal), importance.
impt., important.
impvt., improvement.
in., inch; inches.
inc., increase.
Inc., incorporated.
incog., incognito (in secret).
ince., insurance.
incumbs. (legal), incumbrances.
indemy. (legal), indemnity.
indpt., independent.
in extenso, at full length.
informn. (legal), information.
inhance. (legal), inheritance.
init., *in initio* (in the beginning).
in loc., *in loco* (in its place).
instn., institution.
instns., instructions.
instrons. (legal), instructions.
int., interest.
intdd. (legal), intended.
inter alia, among other things.
interrogs. (legal), interrogatories.
inter se, among themselves.
in trans., *in transitu* (on the way).
inv., invoice.
I.o.M., Isle of Man.
IOU, signed acknowledgment of a debt.
ipso facto, by the fact itself.
i.q., *idem quod* (the same as).
I.R.O., Inland Revenue Office.
I.S.W.G., Imperial Standard Wire Gauge.
ital., italics.
I.W., or **I.O.W.**, Isle of Wight.

J

J.A., Judge Advocate.
J/A, joint account.
J.P., Justice of the Peace.
Jr., Junior.
judgt. (legal), judgment.
judre. (legal), judicature.
Jun., or **Junr.**, Junior.
junc., junction.
jurisdon. (legal), jurisdiction.

K

K.B., King's Bench; Knight Bachelor.
K.B.D., King's Bench Division.
kc., kilocycle.
K.C., King's Counsel.
kg. or **kilo.**, kilogram.
kil., kilometre.
kild., kilderkin.
kl., kilolitre.
kr., Kreuzer (coin); krona; kronen.
kW., kilomatt.
kW. hr., kilowatt hours.

L

£, Pound Sterling.
£E., Pound Egyptian.
£T., Pound Turkish.
L. or **Lat.**, Latin.
L/A, Landing Account; Letter of Authority.
lat., latitude.
lb., (plural lb.), pound weight.
lbl., liberal.
L.C., Lord Chancellor; Lord Chamberlain.
L/C, Letter of Credit; London Clause; London Cheque.
l.c., lower case.
L.C.J., Lord Chief Justice.

L.D., London Docks.
ldg. & dly., landing and delivery.
le. (legal), lease.
led., ledger.
legis., legislature.
L.H.A.R., London, Havre, Antwerp, Rouen (grain trade).
L.H.C., Lord High Chancellor.
L.I., Long Island.
liquon. (legal), liquidation.
L.J., Lord Justice.
L.JJ., Lord Justices.
LL.B., Bachelor of Laws.
LL.D., Doctor of Laws.
LL.M., Master of Laws.
L.M., Long Metre; low middling (cotton).
l.m.c., low middling clause (cotton).
L.M. Region, London Midland Region.
loc. cit., *loco citato* (in the place cited).
loco, on the spot.
long., longitude.
lres. (legal) letters.
L.S., *Locus Sigilli* (place of seal).
L.T.B., London Transport Board.
Ltd., Limited.
ltdg., lighterage.
L.Th., Licentiate in Theology.
L.W.L., load-water-line.
L.W.M., low-water mark.

M

M., Monsieur; thousand (roman numerals).
-/m., thousand (as 20/m).
m., metre; mile; minute.
M/a., my account.
M. or Mk., mark (German coin).
M.A., Master of Arts.
mag., magazine.
maintce. (legal), maintenance.
max., maximum.
M.B., Bachelor of Medicine.
M.C., Military Cross; Master of Ceremonies.
M/C., metalling clause (marine insurance); marginal clause; marginal credit (banking).
m/c, metallic currency; machine.
M.Ch., Master of Surgery.
M.D., Doctor of Medicine; Memorandum of Deposit.
M/d, months after date.
mem. or memo, memorandum.
mentd. (legal), mentioned.
messe. (legal), messuage.
mfg., manufacturing.
mfr., manufacturer.
mg., milligram.
Mgr., Monsignor; Monseigneur.
Michs., Michaelmas.
Mil., milreis (coin).
min., minimum; minute.
min. B/L, minimum bill of lading.
min. wt., minimum weight.
M.I.P., Marine Insurance Policy.
M.J.I., Member, Institute of Journalists.
mkt., market.
Mlle., Mademoiselle.
MM., 2000 (Roman numerals).
M/m, made merchantable.
mm., millimetre.
Mme., Madame.
Mngr., Monsignor.
M.O., Medical Officer; Money Order.
M.O.O., Money Order Office.
mo., mos., month; months.
M.P., Member of Parliament (plural M.P.'s).
M/R, Mate's receipt.
M.R., Master of the Rolls.
M. Region, Midland Region.
MS., manuscript.
M/s, months after sight.
M.Sc., Master of Science.
MSS., manuscripts.
mt., might.
mtg., meeting.
mtge. (legal), mortgage.
mtgee. (legal), mortgagee.

mtgor. (legal), mortgagor.
mtr., matter.
m/u, making up (price—Stock Exchange).
Mus. B. or **Mus. Bac.**, Bachelor of Music.
Mus. D. or **Mus. Doc.**, Doctor of Music.

N

N., north.
N/A, no advice (banking); new account (Stock Exchange).
N/a, non-acceptance.
N.A.A., not always afloat (chartering).
N.B., *nota bene* (mark well—take note); New Brunswick.
N/C, new charter; no charge.
N.C.V., no commercial value.
N.D., not dated.
N.e. or **n.e.**, not exceeding.
N/E, no effects (banking).
necy. (legal), necessary.
nem. con., *nemine contradicente* (no one contradicting).
N.E. Region, North Eastern Region.
n.e.s., not elsewhere specified.
net, lowest; not subject to discount.
N.F., Newfoundland.
N/f., no funds (banking).
nil, nothing.
N.J., New Jersey.
N/m, no mark (shipping).
n/n, no number (shipping).
N/N, not to be noted (Bills of Exchange).
N/O, no orders (banking).
N.o.e., not otherwise enumerated.
Nom., nominal.
Nom. Cap., nominal capital.
non seq., *non sequitur* (it does not follow).
N.o.p., not otherwise provided.
N.O.R., not otherwise rated (shipping).
Nos., numbers.
notwstg. (legal), notwithstanding.
N.P., Notary Public.
n.p., new paragraph.
N/R, not reported (vessel not reported at Custom House).
N.R., no risk (insurance).
N/S, not sufficient funds (banking).
N.S.P.C.C., National Society for the Prevention of Cruelty to Children.
N.S.W., New South Wales.
N.t., new terms (grain trade).
N.T., New Testament.
nt. wt., net weight.
N.U.J., National Union of Journalists.
N.U.T., National Union of Teachers.
N.Y., New York.
N.Z., New Zealand.

O

o., of.
O/a, on account of.
O/A, outstanding account (a dock term).
obdt., obedient.
objn., objection.
obs., observe; obligations.
observon. (legal), observation.
obtd. (legal), obtained.
O/c, old charter; old crop.
o/c, overcharge; out of charge (Customs).
O.C., Open Charter.
O.c. B/L, Ocean bill of lading.
occupon. (legal), occupation.
O/d, on demand.
O/D, overdraft.
O/D., ordinary seaman.
O.D.O., Outdoor Officer (Customs).
O.E., Old English.
O.F., Old French.
offl., official.
O.H.M.S., On Her Majesty's Service.
O.K., widely used slang abbreviation for "All correct".

O.M., Order of Merit; old measure.
O/o, to the order of.
o.p., overproof; out of print.
O.P., open policy (marine insurance).
op. cit., *opere citato* (in the work quoted).
opn., opinion.
oppy., opportunity.
O.R., owner's risk; Official Receiver.
or. (legal), other.
O.R.B., owner's risk of breakage.
O.R.C., owner's risk of chafing.
O.R.D., owner's risk of damage.
ord. or ordy., ordinary.
O.R.F., owner's risk of fire.
ors., others.
O/s., on sale; out of stock; old style.
O.S., Ordnance Survey; Old Saxon; old style; out-size; ordinary seaman.
o/t, old terms (grain trade).
Oxon., of Oxford; Oxfordshire.
oz., ounce or ounces.

P

p., per; page.
Pa., Pennsylvania.
p.a., per annum.
P/A, Power of Attorney.
P.A. or P/av., particular average.
P. & L., Profit and Loss.
pan., panoramic.
par., paragraph; parallel; parenthesis.
para., paragraph.
parcht. (legal), parchment.
parlars. (legal), particulars.
P.C., Privy Councillor; Privy Council; Peace Commissioner (Irish Free State); Police Constable; postcard.
P/C, Prices Current; Petty Cash.
Pc., piece; prices.
P.C.B., Petty Cash Book.
pchsr. (legal), purchaser.
pcl., parcel.
pcs., pieces.
pd., paid.
pecy. (legal), pecuniary.
Per Ann. or p.a., per annum.
per capita, by the head.
perfce. (legal), performance.
per mille, by the thousand.
per pro. or p.p., *per procurationem* (on behalf of).
persl. (legal), personal.
Ph.D., Doctor of Philosophy.
pk., peck; park.
pkgs., packages.
P.L., partial loss (insurance).
P.L.A., Port of London Authority.
plf., plaintiff.
P/m, put of more (Stock Exchange).
pm., premium.
p.m., *post meridiem* (after midday).
P.M., Paymaster; Post-Master.
P.M.G., Postmaster-General; Paymaster-General.
P/N, promissory note.
P.O., Post Office; petty officer; postal order.
P.O.B., Post Office Box.
P.O.C., Port of call.
P.O.Q., Passing over Quay.
posn. (legal), position.
posson. (legal), possession.
pp., pages.
p.p., picked ports (chartering); particular port; *per procurationem* (on behalf of).
P.P., parcel post; post paid.
Ppd., prepaid.
P.P.I., policy proof of interest (marine insurance).
PPS., a second postscript.
ppse. (legal), purpose.
ppt., prompt loading.
P.R., parcel receipt.
P/R, provisional release (shipping).
pr., pair; price; pairs.
Pref., Preference.

premes. (legal), premises.
Pres., President.
prima facie, at first sight.
prodon. (legal), production.
pro and con., for and against.
prodre., procedure.
Prof., Professor.
pro forma, as a matter of form.
prosecon. (legal), prosecution.
pro tem., *pro tempore* (for the time being).
provo. (legal), proviso.
provons. (legal), provisions.
prox., *proximo* (next month).
PS., postscript.
P.S., Privy Seal.
Ps., Psalm; Psalms.
P/S, public sale.
PSS., postscripts.
Pt., point: Port; pint.
P.T., parcel ticket.
pt., part.
P.T.O., please turn over.
Pun., puncheon.
pursce., pursuance.

Q

Q., Qu., query; question.
Q.C., Queen's Counsel.
Q.B.D., Queen's Bench Division.
Q.E.D., *quod erat demonstrandum* (which was to be demonstrated).
qly., qlty., quality.
Q.M.G., Quartermaster-General.
qr., quire; quarter; quarterly.
qrs., quarters.
qt(s)., quart(s).
qto, quarto (4to).
qty., quantity.
quasi, as if.
quesn., question.
q.v., *quod vide* (which see).
qy., query.

R

R., rupees; rouble.
R/A, refer to acceptor.
R/D, refer to drawer (banking).
R.D.C., running-down clause (insurance); Rural District Council.
re, in the matter of.
R.E., Railway Executive.
recd., received.
rect. (legal), reciting.
recomdn., recommendation.
redemon. (legal), redemption.
ref., refce., reference.
reg., regd., registered.
regulon. (legal), regulation.
remr. (legal), remainder.
reqd. (legal), required.
requns. (legal), requisitions.
residy. (legal), residuary.
resply. (legal), respectively.
respt. (legal), respondent.
retd., returned.
revon. (legal), reversion.
revocon. (legal), revocation.
R.L.S., Returned Letter Section.
rm., ream.
R.N., Royal Navy.
R.N.R., Royal Naval Reserve.
R.N.V.R., Royal Naval Volunteer Reserve.
R.O., Reaching Office; Royal Observatory.
R.O.B., remaining on board for exportation (cargo).
Rotn. No., rotation number.
R.P., reply paid.
r.p., return of post.
r.p.m., revolutions per minute.
R.R., Railroad.
Rs., rupees.
R.S., Royal Society.
R.S.O., Railway sub-office.
R.S.P.C.A., Royal Society for the Prevention of Cruelty to Animals.
R.S.V.P., *Répondez, s'il vous plaît* (reply, please).
Rt. Rev., Right Reverend (title of a Bishop).
R.T., Rye Terms.
Rx., tens of rupees.
Ry. or Rly., railway.

S

S, Sulphur.
S/A, (Norwegian) Shipping Co., Ltd.
Salop, Shropshire.
Sarum, Salisbury.
satisfon. (legal), satisfaction.
S.A.V., stock at valuation.
sc., science; scruple (20 grains).
s.c., small capitals (used in proof-correcting).
scp., script.
S/D, sea-damaged (grain).
sd., said.
s.d., *sine die* (indefinitely).
S/E, Stock Exchange.
Sec., **Secy.**, section; secretary.
secy. (legal), security.
Sen., **Senr.**, senior.
seq., *sequentes* (the following).
servt., servant.
settlt. (legal), settlement.
sevl., several.
S.G., Solicitor-General.
S/G, *salutis gratia* (for the sake of safety).
s.g., specific gravity.
sgd., signed.
sh., **shr.**, share.
shd., should.
shl., shall.
signe. (legal), signature.
sine die, indefinitely.
S.I., short interest (insurance).
singr. (legal), singular.
sk(s)., sack(s).
S/L, salvage loss.
sld., sailed.
S/N, shipping note.
S.o., seller's option.
S.O., Sub-office.
Soc., Society.
S.p., supra protest.
s.p., *sine prole* (without issue).
spa. (legal), subpœna.
S.p.d., steamer pays dues.
Spec., speculation.
spl., special.
Spot ship, at place of loading.
Spot, goods in stock; ready for delivery.
S.R., Special Reserve.
S.R. & O., Statutory Rules and Orders.
S. Region, Southern Region.
S/S, **s.s.**, **S**, Steamer; steamship.
St., Saint; street; straits; stet (let it stand).
st., stone (in weight).
s.t., short ton (2000 lb.).
statt. (legal), statement.
Std., standard.
Stg., **Ster.**, sterling.
std. gr., standard gross (10,000 matches).
stk., stock.
stp., stamp.
str., steamer.
subseqly. (legal), subsequently.
substtd. (legal), substituted.
succon. (legal), succession.
sufft. (legal), sufficient.
sums. (legal), summons.
Surv., Surveyor.
survor. (legal), survivor.
sus. (legal), summons.
S.W.G., standard wire gauge.

T

T., ton; tare.
t., the.
T.B., Trial Balance.
T/C, till countermanded (advertising).
T-Cloth, a plain grey cotton cloth (shipping).
T.E., trade expenses.
tenemt. (legal), tenement.
testt. (legal), testament.
testor. (legal), testator.
testrix. (legal), testatrix.
tfer. (legal), transfer.
thabts. (legal), thereabouts.
thby. (legal), thereby.
thfm. (legal), therefrom.
thrin. (legal), therein.
tho., though.
thof. (legal), thereof.
thon. (legal), thereon.

thr., there; their.
thrfr., therefore.
thto, thereto.
T.L., total loss.
T.L.O., total loss only (marine insurance).
T.M.O., Telegraph Money Order.
T.O., Telegraph Office; turn over.
T/O, Transfer Order.
togr., together.
Tonn., tonnage.
T.Q., Tale Quale; *Tel Quel* (grain trade).
T.R., tons registered (shipping).
tr., tare.
Tr., trustee.
Treasr., treasurer.
T.s.s., twin screw steamer.
T.T., telegraphic transfer.
tt., that.
T.Ts., Telegraphic transfers.
T.U.C., Trades Union Congress.

U

U/A, Underwriting Account (marine insurance).
u.c., upper case (capital letters).
u/e, unenumerated (shipping).
U.K., United Kingdom.
ull., ullage.
ult., ultimo (last month).
u.p., under proof (spirits).
u.s., under seal (Customs).
U.S.A., United States of America.
U.S.S.R., Union of Soviet Socialist Republics.
U/w, underwriter.

V

v., versus (against); verse; volt.
Va., Virginia.
valuon. (legal), valuation.
va., volt-ampere(s).
var., various.
V.C., Victoria Cross; Vice-Chancellor.
via, by way of.
vid or **vide**, *vide* (see).
viz., *videlicet* (namely).
vol., volume.
v.o.p., value as in original policy.
vors. (legal), vendors.
vv., verses.
v.v., vice versa.
vy., very.

W

w., with.
W.A.R., with all risks (marine insurance).
W.B., Warehouse book.
W/Bill, Way-bill.
W/b, water ballast (shipping).
Wd., warranted.
wd., would.
w.f., wrong fount (printers' type).
w.g., wire gauge.
wh., which.
whas. (legal), whereas.
whatsr. (legal), whatsoever.
whby. (legal), whereby.
whf., wharf.
whof. (legal), whereof.
whse., warehouse.
whr. (legal), whether.
whrin. (legal), wherein.
W.I., West Indies.
wiht. (legal), without.
witned. (legal), witnessed.
witneth. (legal), witnesseth.
wk(s)., week(s).
wkg., working.
wl., will.
W.O., War Office; Warrant Officer.
W.P., without prejudice.
W.P.A., with particular average.
wr., were.
W. Region, Western Region.
W.S., Writer to the Signet.
ws., was.
wt. or **wgt.**, weight.
W/W, Warehouse Warrant.

X

x.a., ex all.
x.c., ex coupon.
x.d., ex dividend.
x.in., ex interest.
x. new, ex new.
x.r., ex rights.
Xtn., Christian.

Y

Y/A, York/Antwerp Rules (marine insurance).
Y.B., Year Book.
yd., yard.
yday., yesterday.
yieldg. (legal), yielding.
Y.M.C.A., Young Men's Christian Association.
yr(s)., your; year; yours; years.
Y.W.C.A., Young Women's Christian Association.

#, number; numbered (shipping).

INDEX

TYPEWRITING

This book aims, first and foremost, at teaching efficient and accurate keyboard operation at reasonable speeds. Careful attention is also paid to helping the student learn to decipher manuscript, to prepare correspondence and to set out effectively a piece of tabular or display work.

Also in the same series

Shorthand
Book-keeping
Computer Programming
Investment
Origami
More Origami
Karate
Judo
Yoga

and available in Coronet Books